The Fourth Amendment

Other titles in *The Constitution:*

The First Amendment
Freedom of Speech, Religion, and the Press
ISBN: 0-89490-897-9

The Second Amendment
The Right to Own Guns
ISBN:0-89490-925-8

The Fourth Amendment
Search and Seizure
ISBN: 0-89490-924-X

The Fifth Amendment
The Right to Remain Silent
ISBN: 0-89490-894-4

The Thirteenth Amendment
Ending Slavery
ISBN: 0-89490-923-1

The Fifteenth Amendment
African-American Men's Right to Vote
ISBN: 0-7660-1033-3

The Eighteenth and Twenty-First Amendments
Alcohol—Prohibition and Repeal
ISBN: 0-89490-926-6

The Nineteenth Amendment
Women's Right to Vote
ISBN: 0-89490-922-3

The Fourth Amendment

Search and Seizure

The Constitution

Charles M. Wetterer, J.D., Ed. D.

Enslow Publishers, Inc.

40 Industrial Road   PO Box 38
Box 398   Aldershot
Berkeley Heights, NJ 07922   Hants GU12 6BP
USA   UK

http://www.enslow.com

In loving memory of my parents, Katherine Christ and John A. Wetterer.

Library of Congress Cataloging-in-Publication Data

Wetterer, Charles M.
    The Fourth Amendment: search and seizure / Charles M. Wetterer.
      p. cm. — (The Constitution)
    Includes bibliographical references and index.
    Summary: Shows how the Fourth Amendment of the United States Constitution has been historically interpreted by the judicial system and presents cases which illustrate how it is currently being applied.
    ISBN 0-89490-924-X
    1. Searches and seizures—United States—Juvenile literature. 2. United States. Constitution. 4th Amendment—Juvenile literature. 3. Exclusionary rule (Evidence)—United States—Juvenile literature. [1. Searches and seizures. 2. United States. Constitution. 4th Amendment. 3. Exclusionary rule (Evidence)] I. Title. II. Series: Constitution (Springfield, Union County, N.J.)
KF9630.W48   1998
345.73'0522—DC21   97-29946
                              CIP
                              AC

Printed in the United States of America

10 9 8 7 6 5 4

Photo Credits: Coast Guard photo by PA1 F. T. Eyre, p. 42; Collection of The New York Historical Society, p. 22; Collection of the Supreme Court of the United States, p. 61; Courtesy of the Suffolk County Police Museum, pp. 33, 37, 63, 67; Independence National Historical Park Collection, pp. 14, 17, 20, 21, 26; Joseph H. Bailey, Collection of the Supreme Court of the United States, p. 86; National Archives, p. 19; Permission, Cartoon Features Syndicate, pp. 70, 91; Photo by Harris and Ewing, Collection of the Supreme Court of the United States, p. 47; Photo by Richard Strauss and Dane Penland, Smithsonian, Collection of the Supreme Court of the United States, p. 90; Photo by Robert S. Oakes, Collection of the Supreme Court of the United States, p. 49; Suffolk County Police Department, photo by Ben Chiaramonte, pp. 39, 82.

Cover Photo: Suffolk County Police Department, photo by Ben Chiaramonte

Contents

Acknowledgments. . . . .　6

1　*New Jersey* v. *T.L.O.* . . . .　7

2　Historical Background on the Fourth Amendment . . . .　11

3　The Constitution and the Bill of Rights . . . .　15

4　Early Fourth Amendment Cases. . . . .　23

5　Later Cases and the Exclusionary Rule . . . .　31

6　Extending the Exclusionary Rule . . . .　44

7　Warrantless Searches and the Fourth Amendment . . . .　59

8　Search and Seizure in Public Schools . . . .　75

9　Looking Toward the Future . . . .　89

The Constitution. . . . .　93

Chapter Notes 117

Glossary. 123

Further Reading. 126

Index 127

Acknowledgments

Many people helped me with this book. I want to thank Carroll Kelly, director of the Huntington, New York, Public Library and her staff; Nan Peel, director of the Center Moriches, New York, Public Library and her staff; Suffolk County, New York, Police Commissioner John Gallagher and his staff, especially Cecilia M. Clausing, public relations assistant, and Officer Ed Johntry of the Suffolk County Police Museum.

Special thanks to my sister-in-law, Mary V. Reilly, Esq., and my daughter, Katherine W. Eason, Esq., who read and commented on the manuscript. And finally, my heartfelt appreciation to my wife, Margaret K. Wetterer, for her support and assistance throughout the writing of the book.

New Jersey v. T.L.O.

On March 7, 1980, at Piscataway High School in Middlesex County, New Jersey, a teacher came upon two girls smoking in the girls' bathroom. The teacher brought the girls to Assistant Vice Principal Theodore Choplick. He asked them if they had been smoking. One of the girls admitted that she had been smoking, and Mr. Choplick gave her a three-day suspension from school.

The other girl, a fourteen-year-old whose initials were T.L.O., denied smoking. She told Mr. Choplick that she did not smoke, and had not been smoking in the girls' bathroom. Mr. Choplick then asked her to come with him to his office. There he demanded her purse, opened it, and saw a pack of cigarettes and cigarette rolling papers. He now suspected her of using marijuana, an illegal drug. Mr. Choplick thoroughly searched T.L.O.'s purse. He found some marijuana, empty plastic bags, a pipe, a number of one-dollar bills, a list of people who owed her money, and letters indicating that she was selling marijuana.

Mr. Choplick telephoned T.L.O.'s mother and the police. When they arrived at the school, he turned over to the police all the evidence he had taken from the purse. The police asked T.L.O. and her mother to come to police headquarters. During questioning by the police, T.L.O. admitted she had been selling marijuana at the high school.

T.L.O. was suspended from school for three days for smoking in the girls' bathroom. She also received a seven-day school suspension for possession of marijuana. Her lawyer went to the New Jersey State Superior Court. He objected to the seven-day suspension. He claimed it was based on evidence seized in violation of the Fourth Amendment to the United States Constitution. The Fourth Amendment states:

> The right of the people to be secure in their persons, houses, papers, and effects, against unreasonable searches and seizures, shall not be violated, and no Warrants shall issue, but upon probable cause, supported by Oath or affirmation, and particularly describing the place to be searched, and the persons or things to be seized.[1]

T.L.O.'s lawyer told the court that Mr. Choplick's search of her purse did not meet the standards of the Fourth Amendment. There had been no search warrant. There was no probable cause supported by oath to allow such a search. The judge in Superior Court agreed.[2] He found Mr. Choplick's search of T.L.O.'s purse violated the Fourth Amendment. Therefore, he removed the seven-day suspension imposed by the school district.

However, on the basis of the evidence collected by Mr. Choplick when he searched T.L.O.'s pocketbook, the local district attorney brought delinquency charges against T.L.O. in juvenile court. Here, the

judge found that the search was reasonably made on
school grounds by a school authority. It was not in
violation of the Fourth Amendment. He accepted the
evidence taken from T.L.O.'s purse and she was found
guilty of juvenile delinquency and sentenced to a year
on probation.[3]

T.L.O.'s lawyer appealed this decision to the
Appellate Division. This higher court agreed with the
juvenile court decision that the search was not in
violation of the Fourth Amendment.[4] It met the
standard required for school searches. However, the
Appellate Division held that T.L.O. might not have
been advised of her Fifth Amendment rights. She
might not have been aware of her right to remain
silent and not to incriminate herself, before being
questioned at the police station. Therefore, the
Appellate Division ordered the case back to juvenile
court for a new trial. Instead, T.L.O.'s lawyer appealed
the decision to the New Jersey Supreme Court, the
highest court in New Jersey. The appeal was based on
the ground that Mr. Choplick's search of T.L.O.'s
purse had been illegal. The New Jersey Supreme Court
agreed and reversed the decision of the Appellate
Division.[5] It found that the search was unreasonable
and in violation of the Fourth Amendment. It ordered
that the evidence found in T.L.O.'s purse be
suppressed. It could not be used against her in court.
The court reasoned that Mr. Choplick's initial search
of T.L.O.'s pocketbook was unjustified. Finding or not
finding cigarettes in the purse would not prove or
disprove that she had been smoking. In addition, at
the time of the original search, there was no evidence
that a crime had been committed. There was only
suspicion that a school rule might have been broken.

The New Jersey state attorneys appealed the

decision of the New Jersey Supreme Court to the United States Supreme Court—the highest court in the land. The only point in question was whether the evidence seized by Mr. Choplick should not be allowed to be used in juvenile court. The attorneys for the state did not dispute the decision by the New Jersey Supreme Court, that the search was unlawful. The United States Supreme Court granted *certiorari*. That is, it agreed to hear the case.[6] Its 1985 decision in *New Jersey* v. *T.L.O.* would become a landmark decision. It was a case of great importance in establishing a legal precedent on the searching of students by public school officials.[7] Since this was a decision by the United States Supreme Court, the highest court in the nation, all state and federal courts would have to follow it in the future. What would its decision be?

In Chapter 8 we will see what the United States Supreme Court decided in this landmark case on search and seizure in public schools. We will also find out why students in schools may be treated differently from other citizens under the Fourth Amendment. But first, we will see why the men who wrote the United States Constitution believed there was a need for the Fourth Amendment and how it became law. We will examine some important court cases involving search and seizure. We will trace how the courts' interpretation of the Fourth Amendment has evolved, developed, and in some ways changed over the years. Finally, we will come to understand how the Fourth Amendment protects United States citizens and affects our lives.

Historical Background on the Fourth Amendment

The Fourth Amendment to the United States Constitution states:

> The right of the people to be secure in their persons, houses, papers, and effects, against unreasonable searches and seizures, shall not be violated, and no Warrants shall issue, but upon probable cause, supported by Oath or affirmation, and particularly describing the place to be searched, and the persons or things to be seized.[1]

Why did the men who wrote the United States Constitution believe that citizens needed the Fourth Amendment?

As early as the sixteenth century in England there were legal papers called general warrants. These warrants allowed government agents to search any person or premises and seize illegal material.[2] This power to search and seize enabled the government to interfere in many far-reaching areas of citizens' private lives.

For example, the government could control the

press and decide what people could read. Government officials granted licenses only to certain preferred printers. If authorities suspected someone of operating an unlicensed press, they could get a general warrant to search the premises. Government agents might then seize anything they deemed illegal.

Authorities also used general warrants to enforce tax laws. They could search premises if they suspected someone of making or selling taxable goods on which taxes had not been paid. Most English people detested these general warrants. A number of judges, such as Sir Edward Coke, spoke out against general warrants.[3] These judges said that the common law of England gave no power to the government to break in and search any house. The government, however, continued to issue general warrants.

At last, in 1765, an English court issued a landmark decision. It reinforced English citizens' protection rights in matters of search and seizure, and was also the model for the Fourth Amendment to the United States Constitution.[4]

John Entich had written and printed an unlicensed book criticizing the English government. Authorities considered Entich's conduct a rebellion against the government known as seditious libel. It was a criminal offense. They followed the normal practice at the time. A general warrant was issued by Lord Halifax. With the warrant, four agents of the king broke into Entich's house. They ransacked the house and took away many of his private papers and possessions. Entich then sued the king's agents for damages. The agents claimed that the general warrant gave them the right to search. Therefore, they could not be sued. The court disagreed. It awarded Entich damages of three hundred pounds, the equivalent of fifteen hundred dollars. The agents appealed the decision to the English Court of Common Pleas. The appeals court upheld the lower court's decision against the king's agents.[5] The judge, Chief Justice Lord Camden, stated that if the government were allowed to charge any person of committing seditious libel and could issue a search warrant on mere suspicion alone, any house in England could be ransacked by the king's agents. He concluded: If it is law, it will be found in our books. If it is not to be found there, it is not law.[6] This decision has been referred to as "a landmark of English liberty."[7] General warrants were finally abolished in Great Britain in the 1780s.[8]

Earlier, in the mid-1700s in America, British customs officials had a document much like a general warrant called a writ of assistance. It allowed government officials to search colonists' homes and businesses. Writs of assistance were valid for an unlimited period of time. Customs officials used them to help England enforce its trade laws. The writs also were used to stop colonists from smuggling in goods without paying taxes on them.[9] The colonists viewed these writs as tools used by England to enforce unjust laws.

In 1761 in Boston, thirty-six-year-old James Otis quit his post as a king's lawyer in the admiralty court. He was protesting the writs of assistance. Otis made a famous address to the court in February 1761. In it he declared that any act passed by the British Parliament contrary to the natural rights of the American colonists was invalid. He proclaimed:

> . . . A man's house is his castle; and whilst he is quiet he
> is as well guarded as a prince in his castle. This writ, if
> it should be declared legal, would totally annihilate this
> privilege. Custom house officers may enter our house
> when they please . . . . Their menial servants may enter,
> may break locks, bars, and every thing in their way; and

John Adams was the second president of the United States, from 1797 until 1801. He believed that the English writs of assistance were an important reason for the American colonies to declare independence from Great Britain.

whether they break through malice or revenge, no man, no court, can inquire.[10]

Otis failed to stop the issuance of the writs. Colonists, however, recognized him thereafter as a leader of their opposition to oppressive British laws. In 1769 a customs collector who opposed Otis's views viciously attacked him. Otis's crippling injuries forced him to withdraw from public life.

John Adams, a future president of the United States, had been present in the courtroom when James Otis spoke in 1761. Years later Adams described Otis's speech as follows:

> I do say in the most solemn manner, that Mr. Otis's oration against the writs of assistance breathed into this nation the breath of life. . . . [He] was a flame of fire! Every man of a crowded audience appeared to me to go away, as I did, ready to take arms against writs of assistance. . . . Then and there the *Child Independence* was born. In fifteen years, namely in 1776, he grew up to manhood, and declared himself free.[11]

John Adams and others believed that these writs of assistance, were one of the most important reasons for the newly-forming United States to declare independence from Great Britain in 1776.[12]

The Constitution and the Bill of Rights

By the late 1700s, American colonists longed for freedom from Great Britain. They resented the heavy taxes imposed upon them by the British Parliament in which they had no representation. They felt that British laws were trying to take away their God-given rights. The British answer to colonists' complaints and protests was to send more troops to the colonies to enforce these hated laws.

In 1775 fighting broke out between colonists and British soldiers at Lexington and Concord in Massachusetts.[1] Rebellion against British rule quickly spread throughout the colonies. On July 4, 1776, leaders from the thirteen American colonies met in Philadelphia and signed the Declaration of Independence. It was written by Thomas Jefferson. In part, it stated:

> We hold these Truths to be self evident, that all Men are created equal, that they are endowed by their Creator with certain unalienable Rights, that among these are Life, Liberty, and the Pursuit of Happiness.[2]

The American Revolution lasted from 1776 until 1783 when the British finally recognized American independence. During the war, in order to unite the thirteen colonies, John Dickenson and a group of other colonial leaders wrote the Articles of Confederation. The newly-created states approved this document.

It loosely joined the states together to form a weak national government. Under the Articles of Confederation the individual states retained most of the rights to tax, make laws, and enforce them. Congress did not have the power to tax. It had to ask the states for money in order for the national government to function. The central government did not have the money to pay for and develop a strong national army and navy to protect the country. Before Congress could make a law, nine of the thirteen states had to agree to it. In most ways, individual states remained sovereign, independent to govern themselves. By the time the Revolutionary War ended in 1783, many colonists had begun to realize just how ineffective the Articles of Confederation were for the new nation.

An incident in Massachusetts a few years later clearly illustrated the danger of not having a strong central government. In 1786 a group of poor Massachusetts farmers was led by Daniel Shays, a former captain in the Revolutionary War. The farmers rebelled against the state of Massachusetts. They were protesting a state law that would take away their land for unpaid debts. The farmers attacked the courts and the judges. They almost succeeded in taking over the Massachusetts government. Under the Articles of Confederation, Congress was unable to raise an army to stop the rebellion. It was finally put down by the Massachusetts militia. However, Shays' Rebellion showed what might happen unless a stronger central government was formed.[3]

In addition, each of the states mistrusted the other states. States treated each other almost as foreign countries. The restrictions the states put on one another severely hurt trade among the states. National progress was hindered.

Many Americans recognized the need to improve relations among the states and strengthen the central government. James Madison called for a meeting of representatives of the various states. They would make changes in the Articles of Confederation. Delegates met in Annapolis, Maryland, on September 11, 1786. Only five of the thirteen states bothered to send representatives. Alexander Hamilton understood the need for uniting and strengthening the nation. At the conference he encouraged the delegates to call for another meeting in Philadelphia on the second Monday in May 1787. They would amend the Articles of Confederation at this meeting.[4] This time all of the states except Rhode Island sent delegates.[5] A total of

fifty-five leaders came together. After much dissension and discussion, they agreed that they would not try to

James Madison was the fourth president of the United States from 1809 until 1817. He proposed an amendment that would add the Bill of Rights to the United States Constitution in 1789. Madison became known as the Father of the Constitution because of the role he played at the Constitutional Convention in 1787.

amend or change the unworkable Articles of Confederation. Instead, they would write a new Constitution for the United States.

Eventually the delegates decided to establish three different branches of government. These would function as checks and balances on one another. The Congress, the legislative branch, would make the laws. The President, the executive branch, would enforce the law. The Supreme Court, the judiciary branch, would interpret the law. Congress would be composed of a House of Representatives and a Senate. The House would have representatives according to the population of each state. There would be two senators from each state regardless of size.

George Mason had written the Virginia Declaration of Rights and a large portion of the Virginia Constitution itself. He and other delegates at the convention believed that the primary purpose of government was to protect people's rights. These rights included freedom of speech and religion, the right to bear arms, the right to a speedy trial if accused of a crime, and the right to be secure from unlawful searches and seizures.

During the writing of the new Constitution, Mason called for the Bill of Rights to be included. Elbridge Gerry, a delegate from Massachusetts, agreed with Mason. He made a motion to have the Bill of Rights included in the Constitution. Mason seconded the motion. Roger Sherman was a delegate from Connecticut who had helped Thomas Jefferson with the Declaration of Independence. During discussions, Sherman spoke out against the Bill of Rights. Sherman convinced most of the delegates to vote against the motion. He explained that many of

George Mason of Virginia called for the addition of the Bill of Rights to the United States Constitution during the Constitutional Convention in Philadelphia in 1787. He refused to sign the proposed Constitution, primarily because it did not include the Bill of Rights.

the states already had a Bill of Rights in their constitutions.

The majority of the delegates from all of the states supported Sherman's view. However, they agreed that the Bill of Rights should be considered after the Constitution was ratified, officially approved, by the states. When the Constitution was completed, delegates George Mason and Elbridge Gerry refused to sign the document. They objected primarily to the fact that it did not contain the Bill of Rights.[6] Edmund Randolph, a delegate and the governor of Virginia, also refused to sign. He later supported the proposed Constitution, however, at the Virginia ratifying convention. The new Constitution created a strong central government, but it still left substantial power to the individual states.

Each of the states now had to hold a convention to decide whether or not to approve the new Constitution. Delaware was the first state to ratify the Constitution on December 7, 1787. New Hampshire was the ninth state to do so on June 21, 1788.[7] This officially made the Constitution of the United States the supreme law of the new nation.

The fact that the framers had failed to include the

Elbridge Gerry of Massachusetts was another who refused to sign the Constitution because it did not contain the Bill of Rights. He was later vice president of the United States under President Madison from 1813 until 1814.

Bill of Rights in the Constitution, made many of the thirteen states hesitant to ratify it. As soon as the Constitution was finally ratified, a number of states, including Massachusetts, South Carolina, New Hampshire, Virginia, and New York, each submitted a list of rights their state wanted included in the Constitution.

Two states did not ratify the Constitution. North Carolina voted "no." Rhode Island did not even hold a convention to vote. Eventually though, the people in both of these states changed their minds and joined the United States.[8]

The First Congress under the new Constitution met in 1789. James Madison, in the House of Representatives, proposed a bill of rights amendment to the Constitution. The proposal that would become the Fourth Amendment then read as follows:

> The right of the people to be secured in their persons, houses, papers, and effects; shall not be violated by warrants issuing without probable cause, supported by oath or affirmation, and not particularly describing the place to be searched, and the persons or things to be seized.[9]

Congressman Elbridge Gerry of Massachusetts proposed that the first sentence be changed to read,

This painting by T.P. Rossiter depicts the signing of the United States Constitution in 1787. In its original form, the Constitution did not contain the Bill of Rights that we know today. This made some people hesitant to support its ratification.

"The right of the people to be *secure*, in their persons, houses, papers, and effects, *against unreasonable seizures and searches.* . . ." The House of Representatives approved this change.

Then Congressman Egbert Benson of New York recommended changing the words by *warrants issuing* to read *and no warrants shall issue.* He thought that the original wording was good but not sufficient. The House of Representatives voted against Benson's suggested change by a considerable majority.[10]

The House finished reviewing the proposed amendments. Then all the proposals were turned over to a committee of three men chaired by Egbert Benson. The committee was to arrange the proposed amendments' final form and order. When the proposal that was to become the Fourth Amendment was reported back to the House in final form, it contained the words *and no warrants shall issue.* This was the exact wording that Benson had recommended and the House had rejected.[11]

Egbert Benson, a congressman from New York, made changes in the wording of the Fourth Amendment prior to its passage. Benson served as attorney general of New York State for ten years before becoming a judge in New York.

It is hard to believe that Benson did not notice this error. But apparently the other members of the House of Representatives also did not notice. The House passed this and sixteen other amendments, and sent them to the Senate. The Senate reduced the total number to twelve. Both the Senate and the House of Representatives finally agreed on the twelve amendments. President George Washington sent them to the states for approval. Only ten of the twelve amendments were ratified by the required three fourths of the states. Thus, the Bill of Rights, as the first ten amendments to the Constitution are called, became law on December 15, 1791.[12]

The Fourth Amendment actually offers two guarantees instead of one. First, that no search or seizures shall be made without a warrant. Second, no warrant shall be issued without probable cause, supported by oath. Therefore, a warrant may be held to be invalid if someone can convince the court that the reasons given for the search did not constitute probable cause.[13] The question of what is considered "probable cause" has been, and continues to be, a source of endless debate and legal cases.

Early Fourth Amendment Cases

Article III of the United States Constitution established the United States Supreme Court. The article states in part:

> Section 1. The judicial power of the United States, shall be vested in one Supreme Court, and in such inferior courts as the Congress may, from time to time, ordain and establish. . . . Section 2. The judicial power shall extend to all cases, in law and equity, arising under this Constitution, the laws of the United States. . . . [T]he Supreme Court shall have appellate jurisdiction, both as to law and fact. . . .[1]

The federal court system has three levels. On the lowest level the United States District Courts hear cases that arise under federal law. A person dissatisfied with the decision at the District Court level may appeal to a United States Court of Appeals. It is often referred to as the Circuit Court of Appeals. There are thirteen circuits, that is, regional divisions throughout the United States. A final appeal could be made to the United States Supreme Court.

The size of the United States Supreme Court is determined by Congress. When the Supreme Court was established in 1789, it had only six Justices. Since 1869 there have been nine Justices on the United States Supreme Court.[2]

Most of the state court systems also have three levels. Courts of original jurisdiction are the lower courts where a case will begin. People may then appeal to an intermediate appeals court. The state's highest court is the next level of appeal. The names of the state courts vary from state to state. Appeals to the United States Supreme Court may also be made from the highest state courts if a federal or constitutional issue is involved. A decision from the United States Supreme Court is binding on all other courts, both federal and state. However, the opinions of the nine United States Supreme Court Justices rarely are unanimous.

The First Cases Under the Fourth Amendment

The states ratified the Bill of Rights in 1791. For the next fifteen years, no cases involving search and seizure under the Fourth Amendment reached the United States Supreme Court. The very first United States Supreme Court decision involving this amendment took place in 1806. It was called *Ex parte Burford*.[3] The term *ex parte* means there is only one party involved in the case.

John A. Burford was a bad-tempered merchant. He provoked his neighbors and customers in Alexandria, Virginia, so much that they took their complaints to fourteen justices of the peace. These justices issued a warrant for his arrest. It stated in part:

> Greeting: Forasmuch as we are given to understand, from the information, *testimony* and complaint of *many*

credible persons, that John A. Burford, of the said county, shopkeeper, *is not of good name and fame*, nor of honest conversation, but an evil doer and disturber of the peace of the United States, so that murder, homicide, strifes, discords, and other grievances and damages, amongst the citizens of the United States, concerning their bodies and property, *are likely to arise thereby.*[4]

The justices of the peace required that Burford post a bond of four thousand dollars to assure his good behavior. When Burford was unable to raise the money for the bond, he was arrested and put in jail. Burford felt that his rights had been violated. He claimed that his arrest and jailing were illegal both under the Constitution of Virginia and that of the United States. He appealed to the Federal Circuit Court.

This court denied his petition for release. It did, however, reduce the bond to one thousand dollars. Meanwhile, Burford remained in jail. He then appealed to the United States Supreme Court. The Supreme Court agreed with Burford and ordered his release from jail. Chief Justice John Marshall wrote the decision. It stated in part:

> By the [Fourth Amendment] to the Constitution of the United States, it is declared, "that no warrants shall issue, but upon probable cause, *supported by oath or affirmation*." . . . That warrant [arresting Burford] states no offence. It does not allege that he was convicted of any crime. It states merely that he had been *brought* before a *meeting of many justices*, who had required him to find sureties for his good behaviour. It does not charge him of their own knowledge, or suspicion, or upon the oath of any person whomsoever. . . . The *Judges* of this court were unanimously of opinion, that the warrant of commitment was illegal, for want of stating *some good cause certain, supported by oath.*[5]

John Marshall wrote the decision in Ex parte Burford, *the first United States Supreme Court case involving the Fourth Amendment. As the fourth Chief Justice of the Supreme Court (1801–1835) he was principally responsible for developing the power of the Supreme Court.*

The warrant for Burford's arrest did not specify what Burford had actually done. It was not supported by oath or someone's sworn statement as to the necessity for the bond. This first decision by the United States Supreme Court on the Fourth Amendment confirmed that for a warrant to be valid, it must be issued upon probable cause. It must be supported by oath or affirmation. It must give the reason for the warrant. In this case, the Supreme Court did not state exactly what it considered probable cause. However, in 1813, Chief Justice Marshall in *Locke* v. *United States* held that probable cause "is a reasonable ground for belief of guilt."[6] Probable cause for issuance of a search warrant has been described elsewhere as:

> A reasonable ground of suspicion, supported by circumstances sufficiently strong in themselves to warrant a prudent and cautious man in the belief that the person accused is guilty of the offense with which he is charged.[7]

The next United States Supreme Court decision involving the Fourth Amendment was in 1855. In *Smith* v. *Maryland*, the Supreme Court held that the

Fourth Amendment applies only to cases involving federal laws and not to state laws.[8]

Isaac R. Smith was the owner of a ship called *Volant*. He sailed out of the port of Philadelphia, Pennsylvania, and fished along the coast of the United States. In March 1853, Smith was dredging for oysters in the Chesapeake Bay off the coast of Maryland. The sheriff of Anne Arudel County, Maryland, seized Smith's vessel. The sheriff charged that, by dredging, Smith had violated a Maryland law. The law was designed to prevent the destruction of oyster beds. It forbade the taking of oysters with a scoop or drag. The approved method was use of tongs and rakes. The penalty was forfeiture of the boat used in this illegal activity. A justice of the peace found Smith guilty. He ordered the *Volant* forfeited to the State of Maryland. The circuit court of the State of Maryland upheld the decision. Smith appealed to the United States Supreme Court. Smith claimed that the sheriff had seized his boat in violation of the Fourth Amendment.

Maryland law made no provision for an oath or affirmation as to probable cause before issuing the warrant. He further claimed that in his case, no warrant at all was issued. The United States Supreme Court held that the seizure of Smith's boat by the State of Maryland was valid. The Court ruled that the Bill of Rights, including the Fourth Amendment, applied only to the laws of the federal government. It did not apply to the laws of the various states. State laws were not bound by the search and seizure provisions of the Fourth Amendment. The laws of each individual state determined what constituted a valid search and seizure in that state.[9] This interpretation of the Fourth Amendment lasted over one hundred years.

Another Fourth Amendment case, *Murray's Lessee* v. *Hoboken Land and Improvement Company*, was also decided in 1855.[10] The United States Supreme Court ruled that the Fourth Amendment applied only to criminal cases and not to civil actions. In a criminal case the state or federal government initiates legal action against a person for a crime he or she has allegedly committed. In a civil case, one person sues another person to recover damages for a wrong done to him or her. Civil cases are the legal means by which the rights of private citizens are enforced and protected. In the *Murray's Lessee* case, a civil matter, the judge issued a special type of warrant, called a distress warrant, to collect money Murray owed. The warrant had been issued without oath. So, Murray claimed it was not valid. However, the United States Supreme Court stated the Fourth Amendment requirements for a valid warrant applied only in criminal cases and did not apply in a civil matter. This Fourth Amendment restriction to criminal cases is still the law.

Sealed Letters and Packages in the Mail

Ex parte Jackson was decided in 1877. In this case the United States Supreme Court held that sealed letters and packages in the mail were protected by the Fourth Amendment.[11] They could not be opened and inspected by postal authorities without a warrant. The Court said:

> The constitutional guaranty of the right of the people to be secure in their papers against unreasonable searches and seizures extends to their papers, thus closed against inspection, wherever they may be. Whilst in the mail, they can only be opened and examined under like warrant, issued upon similar oath or affirmation, particularly describing the thing to be seized, as is

required when papers are subjected to search in one's
own household.[12]

Early Landmark Decision

Boyd v. *United States* was decided in 1886. It is considered a landmark Fourth Amendment decision.[13]
Congress passed a law in 1874 that said anyone who
brought merchandise into the United States without
paying the lawful custom duties would be fined or
imprisoned. Violators would also be forced to forfeit
the merchandise.

Federal customs officers believed that E. A. Boyd
and Sons had imported thirty-five cases of plate glass
without paying the proper duties on them. Federal
agents seized the glass and arrested the Boyds. They
brought the Boyds to federal district court. In court,
the Boyds were ordered to produce the invoices for
twenty-nine other cases of plate glass they had
received earlier. The government prosecutor needed
these documents to determine the value of the glass it
had seized. The invoices would also help to prove the
government's case against the Boyds. The Boyds
objected to producing the invoices. The court said that
their refusal would be considered a confession to the
charges. So the Boyds handed over the documents.
The government then used the invoices as evidence in
court. The jury found the Boyds guilty. They had to
forfeit the plate glass. On appeal, the Circuit Court of
Appeals upheld the district court's decision. The
Boyds then appealed to the United States Supreme
Court.

The Supreme Court reversed the lower courts'
decisions. It found that the district court's order to
produce the invoices was unreasonable. If the Boyds
had not complied, the district court would have

considered their refusal a confession of guilt.[14] Without the papers, however, the government would not have been able to convict the Boyds. The Supreme Court tied this violation of the Fourth Amendment to the Fifth Amendment's self-incrimination restriction. It found that an unreasonable search and seizure is like a person being forced to be a witness against himself. It stated that the doctrines of both the Fourth and Fifth Amendments apply to all invasions of a person's home by the federal government.[15] The Supreme Court ordered the seized material returned to the Boyds. It did not permit the lower court to allow the use of the contents of an unlawful search and seizure at the criminal trial.[16]

Gradually, in these few early cases involving search and seizure by federal authorities, the United States Supreme Court began to define the protections provided by the Fourth Amendment. The Supreme Court established the fact that the Fourth Amendment applied only to federal criminal cases. It did not apply to civil cases or state courts. These early Fourth Amendment decisions also demonstrated that a person's mail was protected from inspection without a warrant. Unlawfully seized material could also be excluded in court under certain circumstances.

5

Later Cases and the Exclusionary Rule

In the late 1800s a number of laws extended federal control over the sale of drugs and interstate gambling. Then, in 1919, the Eighteenth Amendment was passed. It prohibited the manufacture, sale, or transportation of liquor. The prohibition era of United States history had begun. With these changes, the number of United States Supreme Court cases involving searches and seizures increased dramatically.[1]

Introduction of the Exclusionary Rule

Police in Kansas City, Missouri, believed that Fremont Weeks was illegally using the mail to distribute lottery tickets out of state. On December 21, 1911, without a warrant, police officers went to Weeks's home. They got a key from a neighbor, entered, and searched his house. The police took books, letters, and papers. They turned the seized material over to a federal marshal. The marshal returned to the house with the police and removed lottery tickets and other material. He then turned them over to the federal district attorney.

On the basis of these materials, a federal district court judge ordered Weeks's arrest. Prior to trial, Weeks applied to the court to have his property returned. He claimed it had been illegally seized. The district court issued an order to return the seized material with the exception of the lottery tickets and letters referring to the lottery. This was what the government attorney believed he needed to prosecute Weeks. On the basis of this evidence, Weeks was convicted in federal district court. The court still held, however, that the search and seizure had been illegal.

On appeal, the United States Supreme Court, in 1914 in *Weeks* v. *United States*, reversed the conviction.[2] It stated:

> If letters and private documents can thus be seized and held and used in evidence against a citizen accused of an offense, the protection of the Fourth Amendment declaring his right to be secure against such searches and seizures is of no value, and, so far as those thus placed are concerned, might as well be stricken from the Constitution.[3]

Prior to this decision, the Court had held that illegally seized evidence should not be excluded at trial. The Court had stated that the proper remedy for the person unlawfully searched and or seized would be to sue the offending officers.

This landmark decision carried the *Boyd* decision of 1886 one step further. In *Boyd*, the use of seized evidence was excluded because the lower court unlawfully required the defendants to produce certain invoices. (See Chapter 4.) However, in this decision, for the first time, the Fourth Amendment barred the use of evidence secured through an illegal search and seizure by federal officers. This began what is called the exclusionary rule. The exclusionary rule excludes,

As law enforcement agents began seizing more illegal materials—similar to the gambling equipment of the 1930s, shown here—the number of Fourth Amendment cases in the courts increased.

or omits, from admission in court all evidence gathered by an unconstitutional search and seizure. The *Weeks* decision made it clear, however, that this rule only applied to federal court cases. It did not apply to state courts.

Some states chose to adopt the exclusionary rule in their state courts. Most, however, did not.[4] The majority of the states would not exclude incriminating evidence acquired by unlawful seizures. They did not want to allow criminals to avoid prosecution. If an innocent person was subjected to an illegal search, that person could sue the people responsible for it.

In the *Weeks* case, the Supreme Court also reaffirmed the right of the government to search a legally arrested person. In this way federal officers could discover if the person was armed or in possession of any incriminating evidence of a crime. The evidence could then be seized. This right of a search incident to a lawful arrest has been uniformly maintained in numerous court cases over the years.[5]

Mere Evidence Rule

In January 1918, World War I was raging. The United States, along with Great Britain, France, Russia, Italy, and twenty-three other countries were at war with Germany, Austria-Hungary, Turkey, and Bulgaria. American government authorities suspected that Felix Gouled and two other men, an Army officer and an attorney, were involved in a conspiracy. They were accused of trying to defraud the United States through contracts for military clothing and equipment. The Army officer pleaded guilty and the attorney was found not guilty after a trial.

The Intelligence Department persuaded an Army private named Cohen, a friend of Felix Gouled, to visit his office. He would pretend it was a social call. When Gouled was out of the office, Cohen stole several documents and turned them over to the government authorities. On the basis of these papers, two warrants were issued to search Gouled's office. During these searches government agents seized other papers. When Gouled learned what had happened, he asked for the return of the papers. His requests were denied by the district court. Gouled did not ask for return of the documents that Cohen had stolen. He was not aware that they had been taken until they were presented as evidence against him in court. His objection to their admission during the trial was also denied. He was found guilty. Gouled appealed to the

Circuit Court of Appeals. It referred the case to the United States Supreme Court.

In *Gouled v. United States* in 1921, the Supreme Court declared that none of the documents taken from Gouled's office could be used as evidence against him in court.[6] The searches and seizures were illegal. Private Cohen, without a warrant, had stolen the papers at the direction of the government agents. The Supreme Court declared the papers seized by warrant were also taken in violation of the Fourth Amendment. The warrant was not valid.

The Court held that a valid warrant may not be issued for a search of private papers and materials that are not illegal in themselves. If the materials are not drugs, contraband, or stolen goods, such a search is illegal. The seized materials were simply evidence to be used by the government. The Supreme Court thus began what is now known as the mere evidence rule.

Private Cohen's search of Gouled's office at the urging of an intelligence officer was considered a search and seizure by a governmental agent. However, what if Cohen had entered Gouled's office as a private person and stolen the materials? Could the government have used the materials as evidence in court against Gouled?

Search and Seizure by a Private Person

In *Burdeau v. McDowell* in 1921, the Supreme Court answered this question.[7] A private person stole books and papers and turned them over to an assistant attorney general. The United States Supreme Court ruled that the federal government may use illegally obtained evidence in a criminal trial. As long as it was obtained by someone not connected with law enforcement, this was acceptable. The United States Supreme Court has

been consistent in holding that the Fourth
Amendment does not apply to a search made by a private person.[8] The Fourth Amendment offers
protection *only* against governmental searches.

Automobile Exception or Carroll Doctrine

On September 29, 1921, in Grand Rapids, Michigan,
three prohibition agents posed as whiskey buyers.
They met with George Carroll and two other men. The
men said they had illegal whiskey for sale. However,
they did not have the liquor with them. They said they
would be back with it the following day. The agents
noted the license plate of the car the potential whiskey
salesmen were driving. Perhaps sensing a trap, the proposed sellers never returned.

On October 6 the agents spotted the same car.
They followed but were unable to catch up with it.
Two months later, on December 15, the agents again
saw the car on the road. This time they chased the
car, stopped it, and searched it. When they took apart
the upholstery in the car, they found sixty-eight
bottles of whiskey. Carroll and his passengers were
arrested. He and the other defendants claimed that
the search was illegal. The agents did not have a
search warrant. There was also nothing about the
appearance of the car to indicate that it carried
liquor.

Carroll's lawyers argued that the agents had no
reason to believe Carroll and his friends had
committed a crime. So there was no probable cause to
search the car. Nevertheless, the liquor was admitted
as evidence. Carroll was convicted in federal district
court of possession of illegal whiskey. On appeal, the
United States Supreme Court in *Carroll* v. *United
States*, upheld the lower court's decision.[9] It found:

Law enforcement officers seize illegal whiskey (top) and dismantle a whiskey still (bottom) during the prohibition era of the late 1920s.

That the officers when they saw the defendants believed that they were carrying liquor we can have no doubt, and we think it is equally clear that they had reasonable cause for thinking so. . . . As soon as they did appear, the officers were entitled to use their reasoning faculties upon all the facts of which they had previous knowledge in respect to the defendants.[10]

As stated before, what exactly defines probable cause has been the topic of numerous court decisions. There is no single definition that everyone accepts. In the *Carroll* decision, the court referred to an earlier United States Supreme Court decision that defined probable cause as follows:

If the facts and circumstances before the officer are such as to warrant a man of prudence and caution in believing that the offense has been committed, it is sufficient.[11]

When the United States Supreme Court held that the officers had justification for the search and seizure of Carroll's car, it began what is now known as the automobile exception to the necessity of a warrant. The reasoning is that when an automobile is involved, because of its mobility, there is not usually sufficient time for the law officer to get a search warrant. Therefore, the officers may search the automobile without a warrant when they have probable cause to believe that something illegal will be found there. This Fourth Amendment automobile exception is also known as the *Carroll* doctrine.

Silver Platter Doctrine

Following the *Weeks* decision in 1914, government officials could no longer use illegally seized evidence in a federal court. State courts, however, were not bound by this rule. Most states chose not to accept the exclusionary rule. As a result, federal officials would

Police search an automobile after it has been pulled over and the driver has been questioned. The Supreme Court's decision in Carroll v. United States *gave police the authority to search a vehicle without a warrant as long as they had probable cause.*

often turn over evidence illegally seized by federal agents to state prosecutors. The state prosecutors could then use the evidence in state courts. The evidence was presented to the state prosecutors "on a silver platter." Therefore, this practice was called the silver platter doctrine. The reverse was also true. State officials could give federal agents evidence for use in federal court that would have been illegal for use in the state court.

In 1924 in Des Moines, Iowa, police and federal prohibition agents suspected A. J. Byars of possessing "intoxicating liquors." An Iowa state court judge issued a search warrant. This allowed police to search Byars's house for the liquor. When the state police searched his house, they invited a federal agent named Adams to go with them. During the search they found no liquor. Adams and a state police officer did find counterfeit federal tax stamps. The officer turned over his find to the federal agent. The counterfeit stamps violated federal law but not state law.

With the incriminating evidence, Byars was convicted in federal district court. The decision was upheld by the Circuit Court of Appeals. Byars claimed that the search was illegal. He appealed to the United States Supreme Court. In *Byars* v. *United States* in 1927, the Supreme Court reversed the lower court's decision.[12] It held that the federal agent was participating in the search, not as a private person, but as a federal enforcement officer. The Supreme Court further stated:

> We do not question the right of the federal government to avail itself of evidence improperly seized by state officers operating entirely upon their own account. But the rule is otherwise when the federal government itself through its agents acting as such, participates in the wrongful search and seizure.[13]

In other words, if the state officers had made the search and seizure on their own, and then voluntarily turned over the seized material to federal prosecutors, the material could have been used in the federal court. But in this case, the Supreme Court found that federal agent Adams assisted in the search and seizure by the state officers. Therefore, the exclusionary rule did apply.

Search and Seizure at Sea

In 1927 the United States Supreme Court had to decide whether or not the Fourth Amendment applied to searching an American ship on the high seas, outside the twelve-mile limit of national jurisdiction.[14] Countries have jurisdiction or control of vessels in the waters up to twelve miles from their coastline.

On February 16, 1925, an officer of a United States Coast Guard patrol boat saw a motor boat leave the harbor of Gloucester, Massachusetts. It headed out to sea. Later the officer saw the same motor boat alongside a schooner. It was about twenty-four miles from land. It was also in an area known for switching illegal alcohol to small boats for transport into the state. The officer pursued the motor boat and boarded it. He arrested a man named Lee and two other men. The boat had seventy-one cases of grain alcohol aboard. The boat was seized and taken back to shore. In federal court, Lee was convicted for conspiracy to violate the Tariff and Prohibition Acts.

The Circuit Court of Appeals reversed this conviction. It held that the Coast Guard was not authorized to stop and search a boat that was more than twelve miles from the coast. Therefore, the search and seizure violated the Fourth Amendment. Under the exclusionary rule, the evidence gained from the

United States Coast Guard crewmen bring their inflatable
alongside a thirty-eight foot sailboat to board and search the
vessel. A Coast Guard Cutter stands by in the distance.

illegal search and seizure could not be used against Lee in court. The government appealed, and the United States Supreme Court in *United States v. Lee* reversed the Circuit Court of Appeals. It stated:

> . . . [T]here was probable cause to believe that our revenue laws were being violated by an American vessel and the persons thereon, in such manner as to render the vessel subject to forfeiture. Under such circumstances, search and seizure of the vessel, and arrest of the persons thereon, by the Coast Guard on the high seas is lawful, and like search and seizure of an automobile, and the arrest of the persons therein, by prohibition officers on land is lawful. . . . Moreover search, if any, of the motor boat at sea did not violate the Constitution, for it was made by the [officer] as an incident to a lawful arrest.[15]

The Supreme Court compared this search on the high seas to that in *Carroll*. It extended the automobile exception to American ships at sea. The Court held that the Coast Guard officer had probable cause to believe that Lee was violating the law. Similarly, federal agents had probable cause when they stopped and searched the Carroll automobile.

Prohibition was repealed in 1933. The passage of the Twenty-First Amendment made sale and consumption of alcohol legal again. This ended the many search and seizure cases involving illegal liquor transportation, possession, and sale.

Extending the Exclusionary Rule

In 1949 *Wolf* v. *Colorado* was decided by the United States Supreme Court.[1] The Denver, Colorado, sheriff's office suspected Dr. Julius Wolf of performing abortions. This was an illegal procedure at this time. Without a warrant, a deputy sheriff entered Wolf's office. He removed records that indicated that the doctor was performing illegal abortions. These records were presented in court over Wolf's objection. On the basis of these records, he was convicted. This was affirmed by the Colorado Supreme Court. Dr. Wolf appealed to the United States Supreme Court.

Wolf v. Colorado

In this decision, the Supreme Court held that the Fourth Amendment guarantee against unreasonable searches and seizures was applicable to the states as well as the federal government. The Court also found that the search of Dr. Wolf's office and the seizure of his records were illegal.

However, the Court concluded that the

exclusionary rule was not an essential ingredient of the Fourth Amendment guarantee. The exclusionary rule was a rule of evidence imposed only on federal courts. Although states were bound by the Fourth Amendment, they were not required to follow the exclusionary rule. Therefore, state courts were free to admit or exclude illegally-seized evidence as their state law required.

On this basis, the Supreme Court upheld Dr. Wolf's conviction. As a result of this decision, many state and federal prosecutors continued to make use of the silver platter doctrine. Many people were outraged at a policy that allowed courts to admit illegally obtained evidence on this legal technicality. Nevertheless, this practice went on for almost fifty years.

Finally, in 1956 in *Rea* v. *United States*, the Supreme Court forbade federal officers from offering unlawfully acquired evidence to state officials.[2] This decision eliminated half of the silver platter doctrine. Then in 1960 in *Elkins* v. *United States*, the Supreme Court forbade federal officers from accepting unlawfully acquired evidence from state officials.[3]

The *Elkins* decision at last completely eliminated the silver platter doctrine.[4] It set the stage for a landmark Supreme Court decision the following year in *Mapp* v. *Ohio*.[5]

Mapp v. Ohio

In 1957 three Cleveland, Ohio, police officers arrived at the home of Dollree Mapp. The police thought she was hiding a person wanted in connection with a recent bombing. They also believed they would find evidence of illegal gambling in the house. After telephoning her attorney, Ms. Mapp refused to let the police in without a warrant. The police left, but returned three hours later. They forcibly opened the door to gain admittance. Mapp demanded to see the warrant and one of the officers showed a paper to her. When she would not return the paper, the policeman forced it from her and handcuffed her. The police searched the house. They did not find either the person they were looking for or evidence of illegal gambling. However, they did find illegal obscene materials, lewd books, and pictures. They arrested Mapp. Then Mapp's attorney arrived at the house. One of the policemen told him they had a search warrant, but the officer refused to show it.

At the trial no warrant was ever produced. The court held that the police did not have a valid warrant for the search. Nevertheless, the court decided that under Ohio law, even though the search and seizure had been unlawful, the illegal obscene materials were still admissible in a state criminal prosecution. Mapp was found guilty. Her conviction was affirmed by both the Ohio Court of Appeals and the Supreme Court of Ohio. Dollree Mapp appealed to the United States Supreme Court.

In a 5–4 decision, the Supreme Court held that evidence seized in violation of the Fourth Amendment is inadmissible in a state court—just as it is in a federal court.

In this landmark decision, the Supreme Court overruled *Wolf*. It held that the Fourteenth Amendment, which guarantees due process and equal protection, makes the Fourth Amendment applicable to the states with the same force and effect. The exclusionary rule, which did not allow illegally obtained evidence to be used in federal court, now finally also applied to state courts.

William O. Douglas was appointed to the United States Supreme Court by President Franklin D. Roosevelt. He served as an Associate Justice from 1939 until 1975. He was known for his liberal leanings.

Justice William O. Douglas, in a concurring opinion, stated:

> Once evidence, inadmissible in a federal court, is admissible in a state court a "double standard" exists which, as the Court points out, leads to "working arrangements" that undercut federal policy and reduce some aspects of law enforcement to shabby business. The rule that supports that practice does not have the force of reason behind it.[6]

The Court reversed Dollree Mapp's conviction for possession of obscene literature.

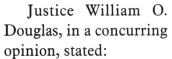 Two-Pronged Test

The exclusionary rule had applied to federal courts since 1914. Its full impact, however, was only felt after the *Mapp* decision extended the rule to all state criminal cases. There now were many more Fourth Amendment cases involving the exclusionary rule. Following *Mapp*, the United States Supreme Court strictly enforced the exclusionary rule. Even the slightest error on the part of the police in obtaining evidence excluded it from being used in court. In *Aguilar* v. *Texas* in 1964 and *Spinelli* v. *United States* in 1969, the United States Supreme Court reversed two decisions where police had actually obtained search warrants.[7] With these decisions, the Supreme Court set up a two-pronged test to determine if there was probable cause for a judge to issue a valid search warrant. The Supreme Court held that in order for any warrant to be valid, it must:

(1) Provide the basis of informant's knowledge of a criminal activity.

(2) Provide sufficient facts to establish the reliability of the informant's report.[8]

Invalid Warrant

In 1964 police in Manchester, New Hampshire, suspected Edward Coolidge of killing a fourteen-year-old neighbor, Pamela Mason. They had probable cause to get a warrant to search Coolidge's 1951 Pontiac. The New Hampshire attorney general, who was also a justice of the peace, issued the search warrant. (Justices of the peace were authorized to issue search warrants in New Hampshire.) Police discovered incriminating evidence in the car, and Coolidge was found guilty of murder in the state court. The New Hampshire Supreme Court upheld his conviction. However, in a 5–4 decision in 1971, the United States Supreme Court in *Coolidge* v. *New Hampshire* reversed the New Hampshire Supreme Court.[9] The United States Supreme Court held that the warrant was invalid. It was issued by a justice who was also a law enforcement officer rather than by a neutral judicial officer. Coolidge's conviction was reversed. The matter was returned to the New Hampshire courts for retrial.

In the years following the *Mapp* decision in 1961, a series of state and federal decisions involving search and seizure were reversed by the United States Supreme Court. In each case the exclusionary rule was applied and the incriminating evidence could not be used in court.[10]

The increase in crime throughout the United States during these same years was blamed in part on the rigid restrictions put on the police and law enforcement agents by *Mapp* and other decisions by the United States Supreme Court. Growing public concern over crime sparked heated debates. The problems with the exclusionary rule were discussed. Many people called for modification of the rule.

In 1971, Chief Justice Warren Burger expressed very strong opposition to the exclusionary rule. He stated that:

> Some clear demonstration of the benefits and effectiveness of the exclusionary rule is required to justify it in view of the high price it extracts from society—the release of countless criminals.[11]

The Chief Justice did not feel that known criminals should go free on the basis of a technical defect in the warrant or a minor mistake by a police officer in attempting to do his or her job to protect the public. He felt that these "honest mistakes were treated in the same way as deliberate and flagrant . . . violations of the Fourth Amendment."[12] Continued

Warren Burger was the fifteenth Chief Justice of the United States Supreme Court. He was appointed by President Richard Nixon and served from 1969 until 1986. Burger expressed very strong opposition to the exclusionary rule.

criticism of the exclusionary rule by Burger and others helped lead to a series of exceptions to the exclusionary rule in later decisions by the Supreme Court.

Two-Pronged Test Abandoned

On the basis of an anonymous letter received on May 3, 1978, the Bloomingdale, Illinois, police obtained a warrant to search the trunk of an automobile belonging to Lance and Susan Gates. They found 350 pounds of marijuana and the Gates's were brought to trial. The Illinois courts held the warrant invalid. It did not give the basis of the informant's knowledge. It also did not provide facts to establish its reliability in accordance with the two-pronged test.

The state of Illinois appealed to the United States Supreme Court. In *Illinois v. Gates* in 1983, the United States Supreme Court reversed the Illinois Supreme Court decision.[13] It held that the two-pronged test for determining probable cause in actions involving informants should be abandoned. The Supreme Court now felt that the validity of a warrant should be determined on the basis of the total circumstances involved in the case.

Inevitable Discovery Exception

On December 24, 1968, ten-year-old Pamela Powers disappeared from a YMCA building in Des Moines, Iowa. She had attended an athletic contest there with her parents. Shortly after she disappeared Robert Anthony Williams was seen leaving the YMCA. He was carrying a large bundle wrapped in an Army blanket. A fourteen-year-old boy reported that he had seen two skinny white legs sticking out of the blanket. Police found Williams's car 160 miles from Des Moines in Davenport, Iowa. Investigators also found some of Pamela's clothes and an Army blanket at a rest stop between Des Moines and Davenport.

A warrant was issued and police in Davenport arrested Williams. The Des Moines police came to pick him up. They agreed not to question Williams until he was brought back to Des Moines and his lawyer was present. As the police were driving Williams back to Des Moines, a police officer described to Williams how hard it was on the child's family not to be able to give their daughter a decent burial. He eventually talked Williams into leading them to Pamela's body. Evidence found on the body was used to convict Williams in the Iowa state courts. From prison, Williams petitioned the Federal District Court. He claimed his rights were violated by the state.

The District Court denied the petition. The Circuit Court of Appeals, however, reversed Williams's conviction. It held that the state failed to prove that the police had not acted in bad faith when they talked to Williams during the trip back to Des Moines.

On appeal, the United States Supreme Court in 1984 in *Nix* v. *Williams*, reversed the Court of Appeals decision.[14] It held that the unlawfully obtained evidence was admissible. It would have been discovered ultimately by lawful means when the body was found. This exception to the exclusionary rule is called the "inevitable discovery" exception. It is another example of the Supreme Court's changing attitude toward the earlier strict compliance with the exclusionary rule.

Good Faith Error Exception

The United States Supreme Court in *United States* v. *Leon*, in 1984, held that the evidence seized with a

warrant the police believed to be valid should be
admitted at trial.[15]

On the same day, the Supreme Court again decided
in *Massachusetts* v. *Sheppard*, that evidence should be
admissible where seized under a defective search
warrant reasonably relied on by police.[16]

In other words, in both *Leon* and *Sheppard*, the
United States Supreme Court was saying that an error
in a search warrant obtained in good faith should not
lead to exclusion of the evidence acquired in reliance
on it. The Supreme Court has stated that the purpose
of the exclusionary rule is to deter unreasonable police
searches and seizures. The police should obtain a
search warrant from a neutral judge. It is, therefore, a
logical conclusion that when a police officer does that
in good faith, he or she should not be penalized for the
judge's error in issuing a defective warrant.

Stop and Frisk

In 1968 the United States Supreme Court decided two
cases on the same day that explain the stop and search
exception to the exclusionary rule, and that exclude
evidence gathered in violation to the Fourth
Amendment.

In downtown Cleveland, Ohio, on October 31,
1963, Detective Martin McFadden observed John
Terry and two other men acting suspiciously. On the
basis of his many years as a detective, he surmised that
they were planning a daylight robbery. The detective
stopped and frisked all three men. He found guns on
Terry and one of the other men. Both men were
arrested.

At his trial, Terry claimed that the detective's
actions were illegal. He did not have probable cause to
search and seize Terry's gun. The court denied his

motion to suppress the evidence of the seized gun. Terry was convicted of carrying a concealed weapon. The Ohio Court of Appeals upheld the conviction. The Ohio Supreme Court dismissed Terry's appeal on the ground that "no substantial constitutional question was involved." This meant that the stop and frisk was not a search and seizure under the Fourth Amendment.

Again, Terry appealed, this time to the United States Supreme Court. In *Terry v. Ohio*, the Supreme Court held that the stop and frisk was in fact a search and seize operation covered by the Fourth Amendment.[17] When the officer stopped Terry, it was a seizure of his person. When he frisked Terry, it was a search, and when he took his gun, it was a seizure. However, the court concluded:

> Officer McFadden had reasonable grounds to believe that petitioner [Terry] was armed and dangerous, and it was necessary for the protection of himself and others to take swift measures to discover the true facts and neutralize the threat of harm if it materialized. . . . Such a search is a reasonable search under the Fourth Amendment, and any weapons seized may properly be introduced in evidence against the person from whom they were taken.[18]

The Terry decision confirmed the fact that stop-and-frisk situations are covered by the Fourth Amendment. Only reasonable suspicion of a dangerous situation, rather than actual knowledge or probable cause that a crime has been, or is about to be committed, is required by the police officer to make such a search.

On March 9, 1965, Officer Anthony Martin was patrolling his beat in Brooklyn, New York. He observed Nelson Sibron, a known heroin user, talking with a group of people whom Officer Martin also knew to be narcotics addicts. Later Sibron entered a restaurant and spoke to three more known addicts. Sibron was at a table having pie and coffee when Martin came up and ordered him to come outside.

Once outside, the officer said to Sibron, "You know what I'm after." Sibron reached into his pocket, and Officer Martin quickly put his hand into the same pocket, taking out several envelopes of heroin. Sibron was arrested. At trial, the court denied Sibron's motion to suppress the seized heroin. He was convicted of unlawful possession of heroin. After Sibron served his sentence, the Appellate Division and the Court of Appeals both upheld the conviction. Sibron appealed to the United States Supreme Court.

The Supreme Court in 1968 in *Sibron* v. *New York*, held that the heroin was not admissible as evidence against the defendant.[19] There was a lack of probable cause to arrest him. The police officer had searched only for narcotics and not for a weapon. Therefore, the officer was not acting in self-defense. In other words, the Court held that a police officer may not stop and frisk a person unless he or she has reason to believe that the person is armed and that the officer or the public would be in danger if the person was not searched. In Sibron's case, the policeman did not think that Sibron was armed and dangerous. He also did not believe he or anyone else was in any danger. Therefore, the police officer could not arrest Sibron without probable cause, which he did not have.

The distinction between the *Terry* decision and the *Sibron* decision is clear. According to the Supreme Court, a police officer may lawfully stop and frisk a suspect *only* when the officer is concerned for his or her own safety or the safety of others.

Suspect Discarding Evidence

Late at night in April 1988, Oakland, California, police officers Brian McColgin and Jerry Pertoso were patrolling in an unmarked police car. They saw a group of teenagers near a small red car parked at the curb. As soon as the youths saw the officer's car approaching, they ran. The red car sped away. The suspicious police officers gave chase.

Officer McColgin drove after the car and Officer Pertoso ran after two of the boys. When one of the boys saw Officer Pertoso almost upon him, he tossed away what appeared to be a rock. Shortly after, Officer Pertoso tackled the suspect, handcuffed him, and radioed for assistance.

When other police arrived, they searched the suspect. They found he had $130 in cash and a pager, an electronic device by which he would receive a signal if someone were trying to contact him. The "rock" the suspect had thrown away turned out to be crack cocaine.

In Juvenile Court, the suspect's attorney argued that the cocaine evidence should not be allowed in court. He claimed that his client had been unlawfully seized by Officer Pertoso. When Pertoso chased the suspect, this "show of authority" was considered a seizure according to the *Terry* stop-and-frisk rule. The judge refused to suppress the cocaine evidence and the suspect was convicted.

The California Court of Appeal reversed the conviction. The appeals court held that the suspect had been seized when he saw Pertoso running toward him. Since this "seizure" was unlawful, the cocaine had to be suppressed at trial. The California Supreme Court refused to review the case, and the state of

California appealed to the United States Supreme Court.

The United States Supreme Court, in 1991 in *California* v. *Hodari D.*, reversed the decision of the Court of Appeal.[20] The Court stated that even if the officer's chase was not based on reasonable suspicion, as required by the *Terry* decision, the police officer had seen the suspect toss away the cocaine before he stopped him. The cocaine's recovery was not the result of a search. Therefore, it is not covered by the Fourth Amendment. It was held that since the suspect did not comply with Officer Pertoso's "show of authority," there was no seizure until he was tackled by the police officer.

The United States Supreme Court is saying that when people scatter in panic when the police are sighted, it would be reasonable for the police to stop them, if possible, for a brief inquiry as to why they are running away.

Illegally Searching an Innocent Person

On the morning of November 26, 1965, agents of the Federal Bureau of Narcotics believed they would find illegal drugs in the apartment of Webster Bivens. They entered the apartment and arrested him for narcotics violations. The agents handcuffed Bivens in front of his wife and children. They threatened to arrest the entire family. They then proceeded to search the apartment, but found no drugs.

Bivens was taken to the federal courthouse in Brooklyn, New York. He was interrogated, booked, and subjected to a strip search. The government was unable to prove its case against Bivens. He then sued in federal court for $75,000 in damages. This was $15,000 from each of the agents involved in his arrest.

He stated that the arrest and search were made without a warrant. He also asserted that unreasonable force was used in making the arrest. The entire experience caused him great humiliation, embarrassment, and mental suffering. The Federal District Court dismissed Bivens's claim and the Circuit Court of Appeals affirmed. Bivens appealed to the United States Supreme Court.

The Supreme Court reversed the Court of Appeals. It held that Bivens was entitled to recover money damages for injuries he suffered as the result of the agents' violation of his Fourth Amendment rights.[21] However, in later cases decided by the Supreme Court, federal officers were held *not* liable to be sued personally in such instances.

Qualified Immunity

On November 11, 1983, Russell Anderson and other agents from the Federal Bureau of Investigation (FBI) believed that a man suspected of a bank robbery was hiding in the home of Robert Creighton, Jr. They forced their way into Creighton's home and searched it. The suspected bank robber was not there. Creighton sued Anderson and the other agents in Federal District Court. The agents claimed that they had qualified immunity. They could not be sued personally if they were acting in good faith. The Federal District Court judge agreed and granted summary judgment to the FBI agents.

Summary judgment is given on the basis of the information presented without a trial. The judge held that the agents were justified in making the search since they had probable cause to search Creighton's house at once. They did not have time to get a search warrant.

The Circuit Court of Appeals reversed on the ground that the judge could not award the agents summary judgment. The agents would have to prove during a trial that they had probable cause and there was the need to search the house immediately. The Court of Appeals further said that the agents were not entitled to qualified immunity. They could be sued for their actions. The agents appealed to the United States Supreme Court.

In *Anderson* v. *Creighton,* the Supreme Court reversed the judgment of the Court of Appeals.[22] It held that a federal officer who conducts a warrantless search in violation of the Fourth Amendment cannot be held personally liable for money damages if it is found that a reasonable officer could have believed the search to be lawful under the Fourth Amendment.

Warrantless Searches and the Fourth Amendment

When the Fourth Amendment became law in 1791, no one could have anticipated that listening to other people's telephone calls might someday be a violation of its provisions.

Wiretapping Cases

In 1928 the United States Supreme Court was confronted with its first Fourth Amendment wiretapping case in *Olmstead* v. *United States*.[1] Roy Olmstead was a former federal agent. He controlled a huge illegal liquor operation in Seattle, Washington. It was almost impossible for the government to get evidence to convict him of violating the law. Olmstead had contacts on the Seattle police force. Friendly law officers would warn him whenever there was to be a raid on one of his warehouses.

Unknown to Olmstead, however, four federal prohibition officers inserted wires along telephone lines from his home and those of other suspects. The agents did not enter any of the houses. They made the taps in the streets near the buildings. Federal agents recorded Olmstead's private conversations and gathered incriminating evidence of the unlawful operation. The federal agents arrested a number of bootleggers and seized many cases of illegal liquor. With the evidence acquired through the wiretapping, Olmstead was convicted in federal district court.

The United States Court of Appeals affirmed the convictions of conspiracy to violate the Prohibition Act. It held that the tapping of the defendant's telephone lines was "an unethical intrusion on the privacies of persons who are suspected of crime." It was not, however, prohibited by either the Fourth or Fifth Amendments. Olmstead appealed to the United States Supreme Court.

The Supreme Court upheld the Court of Appeals decision. Chief Justice William Howard Taft, former President of the United States, held that the Fourth Amendment:

> . . . does not forbid what was done here. There was no searching. There was no seizure. The evidence was secured by the use of the sense of hearing and that only. There was no entry of the houses or offices of the defendants. . . . The language of the Amendment can not be extended and expanded to include telephone wires reaching to the whole world from the defendant's house or office. The intervening wires are not part of his house or office any more than are the highways along which they are stretched.[2]

Four of the nine Supreme Court Justices dissented. They believed that the government agents' actions violated both the Fourth and Fifth Amendments. This decision allowing warrantless wiretapping that did not physically intrude on a person's property continued as law for many years. It was confirmed in 1942 by another Supreme Court decision in *Goldman* v. *United States*.[3]

Expectation of Privacy

The precedent set by *Olmstead* was eventually overturned by the United States Supreme Court in 1967. Agents from the Federal Bureau of Investigation (FBI) suspected Charles Katz of sending betting information over the telephone in violation of federal law. If the agents could have overheard Katz's conversation without a hearing device, his statements would not have been protected by the Fourth Amendment.

The FBI agents had sufficient information and plenty of time to obtain a court order to authorize a warrant for electronic surveillance. They did not bother, however, to get a warrant. Without a warrant, they attached an electronic listening and recording device to the roof of a public telephone booth in Los Angeles. They knew Katz made his calls from there. They recorded Katz's voice as he spoke to people in Miami and Boston about their illegal betting on sports events. Katz was arrested and brought to Federal District court.

Over Katz's objection, the government was permitted to introduce the recordings of Katz's

William Howard Taft was the twenty-seventh president of the United States from 1909 until 1913, and the tenth Chief Justice of the Supreme Court from 1921 until 1930. He was appointed to the Court by President Harding.

end of the telephone conversations at the trial. As a result Katz was convicted in federal district court. The Court of Appeals, relying on the *Olmstead* and *Goldman* decisions, affirmed the conviction. The court held that because the listening device had not been inside the phone booth occupied by Katz, there had been no violation of the Fourth Amendment.[4]

The United States Supreme Court, in *Katz* v. *United States*, disagreed.[5] It held that a search warrant was necessary for this type of electronic surveillance. The Court changed the way in which it described Fourth Amendment protection. It now held that "the Fourth Amendment protects people, not places" from unlawful searches and seizures. In overruling *Olmstead* and *Goldman*, the Supreme Court found that:

> These considerations do not vanish when the search in question is transferred from the setting of a home, an office, or a hotel room to that of a telephone booth. Wherever a man may be, he is entitled to know that he will remain free from unreasonable searches and seizures.[6]

In effect, this decision held that the Fourth Amendment protected the privacy of the person inside the place and not the place itself. Justice John Marshall Harlan, in his concurring opinion in *Katz*, stated that:

> an enclosed telephone booth is an area where, like a home, . . . and unlike a field, . . . a person has a constitutionally protected reasonable expectation of privacy.[7]

Over the years following this decision, a "reasonable expectation of privacy" has become a determining factor as to whether a person is protected by the Fourth Amendment. If a person has a reasonable expectation of privacy in an enclosed area such as a

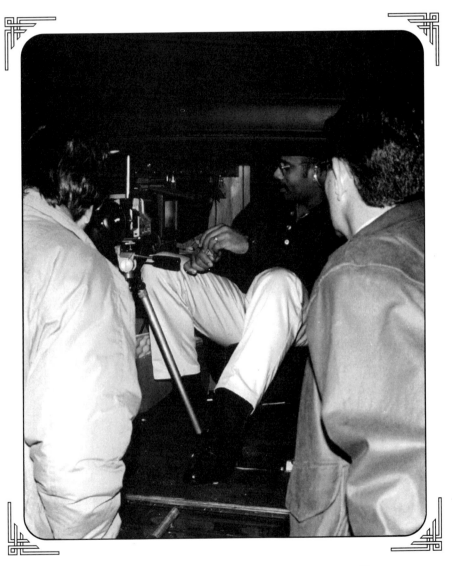

Law enforcement officers conduct electronic surveillance. The Supreme Court, in Katz v. United States, *held in 1967 that a search warrant is necessary to conduct this type of search.*

closed telephone booth, that person is covered by the amendment. However, in the open fields, a person could not have a reasonable expectation of privacy.

Open Fields Doctrine

An early United States Supreme Court decision in 1924 had held that "[C]onversations in the open would not be protected against being overheard for the expectation of privacy under the circumstances would be unreasonable."[8] This became known as the open fields doctrine.

In 1984 in *Oliver* v. *United States*, the United States Supreme Court held that a search of marijuana fields by police officers without a warrant was permissible under the open fields doctrine.[9] Narcotics agents of the Kentucky State police received a report that Ray Oliver was growing marijuana. They went to his farm and found a locked gate with a "No Trespassing" sign. The agents walked along the road and discovered a field of marijuana over a mile from Oliver's house. Oliver was arrested and charged with "manufacturing a controlled substance" in violation of federal law.

The federal district court suppressed evidence of the discovery of the marijuana. Oliver, it said, had a reasonable expectation that the field would remain private. Therefore, the search and seizure had been illegal. The Circuit Court of Appeals reversed. It held that the open fields doctrine permits officers to enter and search an open field without a warrant.

The United States Supreme Court agreed. It held that the special protection accorded by the Fourth Amendment to the people in their "persons, houses, papers, and effects" is not extended to open fields. This only applies to the area immediately around the person's home. A person may not legally demand privacy for activities conducted out-of-doors in fields. The marijuana field was a mile away from the farmhouse. The Supreme Court stated:

> We conclude, from the text of the Fourth Amendment and from the historical and contemporary understanding of its purposes, that an individual has no legitimate expectation that open fields will remain free from warrantless intrusion by government officers.[10]

Searches from the Air

May a person growing marijuana in his backyard have a reasonable expectation of privacy to protect him from an aerial search by police? The following case answers this question.

The Santa Clara, California, police received an anonymous telephone tip that someone named Ciraolo was growing marijuana in his backyard. Ciraolo's yard was enclosed by high fences. This made it impossible to view from ground level. Officers flew over at an altitude of 1,000 feet. They identified marijuana growing in the yard.

A search warrant was obtained on the basis of an officer's naked-eye observations and a photograph of the yard and surrounding area. The police searched the premises and seized the marijuana. Ciraolo maintained he had a reasonable expectation of privacy because his yard was enclosed. The California trial court denied Ciraolo's motion to suppress the evidence. Ciraolo pleaded guilty to a charge of cultivation of marijuana.

The California Court of Appeal reversed Ciraolo's conviction. It held that the warrantless aerial search violated the Fourth Amendment. The state appealed to the United States Supreme Court.

In *California* v. *Ciraolo* in 1986, the Supreme Court,

in a 5 to 4 decision, reversed the California Court of Appeal's decision.[11] It held that the aerial search was reasonable. Chief Justice Warren Burger explained that:

> In an age where private and commercial flight in the public airways is routine, it is unreasonable for respondent [Ciraolo] to expect that his marijuana plants were constitutionally protected from being observed with the naked eye from an altitude of 1,000 feet. The Fourth Amendment simply does not require the police traveling in the public airways at this altitude to obtain a warrant in order to observe what is visible to the naked eye.[12]

In 1989 the United States Supreme Court was faced with another search from the air in *Florida* v. *Riley*.[13] The Pasco County, Florida, sheriff received an anonymous tip that marijuana was being grown in a greenhouse behind Michael Riley's mobile home. The sheriff's office could not obtain a search warrant. The anonymous tip did not give them probable cause to do so. They could not see the contents of the greenhouse from the road, however.

One of the officers circled in a helicopter at four hundred feet over Riley's property. From there, he was able to see with his naked eye what he thought was marijuana growing in the greenhouse. With a warrant based on the officer's observations, the sheriff seized the marijuana. Riley was arrested. The Florida Supreme Court held that the search violated the Fourth Amendment.

On appeal, the United States Supreme Court reversed. Five members of the Court agreed. Riley did not have a reasonable expectation that the greenhouse was protected from observation from a helicopter. Because of this, the helicopter surveillance did not

Police officers leave a police helicopter. The first use of the helicopter by police was in New York in 1947. Today, every state in the country uses helicopters in police work, sometimes in search of hidden marijuana fields that are only visible from above.

constitute a "search" prohibited under the Fourth Amendment.

The first use of the helicopter by police was in New York in 1947. Today every state in the United States uses helicopters in police work.[14]

Current United States Supreme Court decisions do not support the idea that people should be protected by the Fourth Amendment from aerial surveillance. However, it is quite possible that this may change in the future.

Airport Searches

As air travel has become more common, the possibility that someone might place a bomb on a plane or a hijacker might take over control of an airplane at gunpoint has become a reality. In order to protect passengers from these dangers, metal detectors and X-ray machines have been installed at airports. Do these practices involve a search prohibited by the Fourth Amendment?

In 1974 in *United States* v. *Edwards*, the United States Court of Appeals held that such a practice was justified and not in violation of the Fourth Amendment.[15] The Court reasoned that if travelers want to avoid an airport search of passengers and luggage, they can do so "by choosing not to travel by air."[16]

Drug Courier Profile

The United States Drug Enforcement Administration (DEA) wanted to help its agents identify travelers who might be transporting illegal drugs. They worked out a profile on the behavior of people who might do this.

In 1980 in *Reid* v. *Georgia*, the United States Supreme Court held that stopping an airline passenger at an airport because that passenger's conduct fit a "drug courier profile" did not meet the standard of reasonable suspicion of criminal activity, as required by the Fourth Amendment.[17] It held that the agents' search of Reid violated the Fourth Amendment. The seizure of drugs he was carrying was illegal.

Then in July 1984, Andrew Sokolow arrived in Hawaii on the last leg of a return flight from Miami. He collected his baggage and was leaving Honolulu International Airport. DEA agents stopped him because he "had all the classic aspects of a drug courier." The agents knew that:

(1) Sokolow had paid $2,100 for two airplane tickets from a roll of twenty-dollar bills.

(2) He was traveling under a name that did not match the name under which his telephone number was listed.

(3) His outgoing destination was Miami, a source city for illicit drugs.

(4) He had stayed in Miami for only forty-eight hours, even though a round-trip flight from Honolulu to Miami takes twenty hours.

(5) He appeared nervous during his trip.

(6) He checked none of his luggage.

The DEA agents brought in a drug sniffing dog. The dog signaled the presence of drugs. The agents searched Sokolow's carry-on luggage and found 1,063 grams of cocaine. They arrested him. On the basis of the evidence, Sokolow was convicted in Federal District Court.

The Circuit Court of Appeals reversed the conviction. It held that under the Fourth Amendment the DEA agents did not have a reasonable suspicion to stop him. The government appealed to the United States Supreme Court.

In 1989 the Supreme Court in *United States* v. *Sokolow* reversed the decision of the Circuit Court of Appeals.[18] It held that the DEA agents, even without probable cause, can stop and briefly detain a person. This is permissible if they have reasonable suspicion, supported by facts, that criminal activity may be involved.

The apparent change of attitude on the part of the United States Supreme Court from its previous decision in *Reid* may have been the result of the increasing threat of drugs in our society. It may also be

Customs officials have the right to look through the bags of all people entering the United States in search of illegal items being brought into the country.

in response to public outrage in what seems to many people a lack of common sense in deciding what constitutes reasonable suspicion.

Personal Searches and Seizures

Without a warrant, the Los Angeles County Deputy Sheriff and other officers came to the home of Antonio Rochin to arrest him. They suspected him of dealing in drugs. They forced their way into his home. Rochin rushed into his bedroom, quickly grabbed two tablets from a night table, and swallowed them. One officer pounded Rochin on the back. The other officer stuck his fingers down Rochin's throat and tried to make him spit up the tablets. When Rochin did not, they drove him to the hospital and had his stomach pumped. Remains of two capsules of morphine were recovered.

Over Rochin's objection, the California state courts allowed the presentation of the evidence recovered from Rochin's stomach. Rochin was convicted. On appeal in 1952, the United States Supreme Court, in *Rochin* v. *California*, reversed the conviction.[19] Speaking for the Court, Justice Felix Frankfurter stated that the conduct of the police officers "shocks the conscience."[20] The Court considered this search and seizure an extensive intrusion and a serious breach of Rochin's expectation of privacy and a violation of the Fourth Amendment.

In 1966 the Supreme Court, in *Schmerber* v. *California*, concluded that the State may, over the suspect's protest, have a physician extract blood from a person suspected of drunken driving.[21] The Court held that this would not violate the Fourth Amendment's protection against unreasonable search and seizure.

Consider the case of *Cupp* v. *Murphy*, decided by
the United States Supreme Court in 1973.[22] Daniel
Murphy was accused of the strangulation-murder of
his wife. He voluntarily went to the police station. The
police then took fingernail scrapings over his protest
and without a warrant. The scrapings contained traces
of skin, blood cells, and fabric from his wife's
nightgown. Murphy was convicted in the Oregon state
courts of murdering his wife. From prison Murphy
petitioned the Federal District Court on the ground
that he had been illegally convicted in the state courts.
The district court denied his petition but the Circuit
Court of Appeals reversed. It held that taking
fingernail scrapings without a warrant was a seizure in
violation of the Fourth Amendment.

On appeal, the United States Supreme Court found
that the scraping was acceptable because of the
circumstances. There was probable cause to acquire
the fingernail scrapings. There was a very limited
intrusion on Murphy's privacy. Finally, a strong
possibility existed that the evidence might have been
destroyed before a warrant could have been obtained.
The Supreme Court reversed the Court of Appeals.
Murphy's conviction was reinstated.

On the evening of July 18, 1982, Rudolf Lee, with
gun drawn, approached Ralph Watkinson. Watkinson
was closing his shop in Virginia. Lee ordered
Watkinson to freeze. Instead, Watkinson pulled out his
own gun and shot Lee. Lee returned the fire and shot
Watkinson in the leg. Lee then ran from the scene.

The police arrived, and Watkinson was taken to
the Medical College of Virginia hospital. Watkinson
was being treated in the emergency room. Meanwhile,
Lee, with a bullet in his left side, came to the same
hospital for treatment. "That's the man who shot me,"

Watkinson declared, as soon as he spotted Lee. Watkinson explained that he had also shot Lee during the attempted robbery. Lee denied everything. He claimed that he had been shot by someone who had tried to rob him. State prosecutors wanted to have the bullet removed from Lee's chest. This would provide evidence of Lee's innocence or guilt. Lee refused to allow them to take out the bullet. A Virginia state court, however, granted a motion to force Lee to have the bullet removed. A Federal District Court enjoined (stopped) the threatened surgery. The Circuit Court of Appeals upheld the decision. The state appealed to the United States Supreme Court.

In 1985 the Supreme Court, in *Winston* v. *Lee*, agreed with the lower courts' decisions.[23] It held that the surgery to Lee would be an unreasonable search under the Fourth Amendment. The surgery would intrude substantially on Lee's reasonable expectation of privacy. The state failed to prove to the court a compelling need for the bullet as evidence. The state could bring their case against Rudolf Lee without it.

These personal search and seizure cases indicate that the defendant's expectation of privacy and the degree of intrusion caused by the search are weighed against the governmental interest in the search.

Suspicionless Drug Testing

In 1989 the United States Supreme Court, in *Skinner* v. *Railway Labor Executives' Association*, held that individualized suspicion to test employees for drugs is not required when there are compelling government interests involved.[24] In this case, there was evidence that alcohol and drug abuse by railroad employees posed a threat to public safety.

Again in *National Treasury Employees Union* v. *Von*

Raab, the Supreme Court held that the suspicionless drug testing of customs agents in positions where they handled drugs and carried firearms was reasonable under the Fourth Amendment.[25] The governmental interest in such testing outweighed the employees' privacy expectations.

In 1990 Georgia passed a law requiring candidates for state offices to pass a drug test before they could be placed on the ballot. Walker L. Chandler was the Libertarian Party candidate for lieutenant governor in 1994. He objected to the test. However, he took the test under protest and passed it. He then brought an action against the state arguing that the law violated the Fourth Amendment. Both the Federal District Court and the United States Court of Appeals found this suspicionless general search constitutional.[26] Their rulings were based on the ground that elected state officials were trustees and servants of the public, and the public had the right to know about candidates' drug use, if any. Candidates for high office can have only a limited expectation of privacy. Financial disclosure and other privacy intrusions are required of candidates for public office.

The State of Georgia admitted that there was no evidence of drug problems by any candidates in the past. Chandler appealed the Court of Appeals decision to the United States Supreme Court. In *Chandler* v. *Miller,* the Supreme Court reversed the lower courts. It found that unlike the findings in *Skinner* and *Von Raab,* Georgia had failed to show a special need to justify the testing.[27]

Search and Seizure in Public Schools

Since the 1960s there have been many court cases throughout the United States involving searches of students in the public schools. Teachers, administrators, and sometimes the police search for drugs and weapons that students may have brought into the schools. How does the Fourth Amendment apply to searches and seizures involving students in public schools?

Locker Searches

In 1966 three detectives from the Mount Vernon, New York, Police Department presented a search warrant to Dr. Panitz, the vice principal of Mount Vernon High School. The warrant authorized a search of two students. The police suspected that the boys were dealing in drugs. They were brought to the vice principal's office and searched, but nothing was found.

The detectives then asked to see the boys' lockers. Dr. Panitz opened one boy's school locker and found marijuana cigarettes. That boy was arrested. The judge found the police search warrant to be defective because it did not include the lockers. Still, the judge allowed the marijuana to be offered as evidence. This was done on the grounds that Dr. Panitz had voluntarily consented to the search of the boy's locker, and he had the right to do so. The appellate court reversed the boy's conviction. It held that since the consent for the search was influenced by the search warrant, the vice principal had not freely given his consent. The New York Court of Appeals reversed the appellate court and reinstated the original conviction.[1] The court held that:

> Not only have the school authorities a right to inspect [the student's locker] but this right becomes a duty when suspicion arises that something of an illegal nature may be secreted there. When Dr. Panitz learned of the detectives' suspicion, he was obligated to inspect the locker. This interest, together with the nonexclusive nature of the locker, empowered him to consent to the search by the officers.[2]

The convicted boy appealed to the United States Supreme Court.[3] In *Overton* v. *New York*, the Supreme Court voided the conviction and sent it back to the New York Court of Appeals for further consideration in light of another United States Supreme Court decision in 1968, *Bumper* v. *North Carolina*.[4]

The *Bumper* decision held that a search cannot be justified as lawful if consent is coerced. In a rehearing of the *Overton* case by the New York Court of Appeals, which is New York's highest court, the court held that the *Bumper* decision was not relevant to this case. Dr. Panitz had obviously consented to the search.[5] He was not coerced by the search warrant. Overton was placed on indefinite probation for up to five years. He appealed again, but the Supreme Court refused to hear the case.[6]

In another school locker search case, the Kansas Supreme Court held that school authorities have the right to search a student's locker without a search warrant if they have reasonable suspicion that the locker contains something that is prohibited.[7]

On the day following a burglary in a music store, two police officers asked a Kansas high school principal to open the locker of a student at the school. With the student's consent, the principal opened his locker. In the locker, the principal found a key to a bus depot locker hidden in the bottom of a pack of cigarettes. Police got a warrant, opened the bus depot locker, and found the items taken from the music store.

The student's attorney objected. He said that the original search of the boy's locker violated the Fourth Amendment. The trial court allowed the contents of the depot locker search to be admitted into evidence, however. The student was convicted of second degree burglary. On appeal, the Supreme Court of Kansas upheld the conviction and said:

> A school does not supply its students with lockers for illicit use in harboring pilfered property or harmful substances. We deem it a proper function of school authorities to inspect the lockers under their control and to prevent their use in illicit ways or for illegal purposes.[8]

The court further held that it is not essential that the student be given a *Miranda*-type warning, telling him he has the right to remain silent, in order for the search to be valid.[9] The United States Supreme Court refused to hear an appeal by the student.[10]

These and other school search cases all support the

idea that the school authorities have the legal right, and in some cases the duty, to search a student's locker.[11] They may also consent to its being searched by the police if there is reason to suspect that something prohibited, illegal, or dangerous is in the locker. In fact, in the case of a dangerous weapon, such as a knife or gun, school officials could be held negligent if they fail to make such a search.[12] This is because of the doctrine of *in loco parentis*, meaning that a school person stands in place of the parent. In addition, the school retains the custody and control of school lockers.

Car Searches on School Property

The school does not own or control student automobiles parked on school grounds. However, the presence of cars on school property brings them under the authority of the school. This is true because the school is responsible for maintaining the safety of the school's immediate surrounding area. When school officials have reasonable suspicion that articles of a dangerous or criminal nature are being concealed in a car on school property, it would seem they have the obligation to call the police or search the automobile themselves. In either case a search could be made immediately without a warrant under the *Carroll* doctrine or automobile exception rule.

Personal Searches

Acting on a tip, the administrator for discipline in a New York high school called one of the students out of the classroom. The student was asked to accompany the administrator to the office. On the way the administrator observed a bulge in the student's left pants' pocket. He also saw the student continually putting his hand in and out of that pocket. When they neared the office, the student suddenly bolted out of the building. The administrator ran after him.

A policeman was stationed outside the building. He asked what was going on. The administrator replied, "He has some stuff on him." They chased the student, and the administrator caught him three blocks from the school. He forced the boy's hand open and found a syringe, an eyedropper, and a hypodermic needle—tools for the injection of drugs.

At this point, the policeman, who also pursued the boy, arrived. The administrator turned over the evidence to the policeman, and the student was arrested. In criminal court, a motion to suppress the seized evidence was granted. The court held that the seizure violated the Fourth Amendment. The state appealed to the New York Appellate Division. The Appellate Division reversed the criminal court decision.[13] It held that the search and seizure by the administrator was reasonable. He suspected that something unlawful was being committed or about to be committed. The administrator, acting *in loco parentis*, was therefore obligated to make the search. In *People* v. *Jackson*, the court said,

> The *in loco parentis* doctrine is so compelling in light of public necessity and as a social concept antedating the Fourth Amendment, that any action, including a search, taken thereunder upon reasonable suspicion, should be accepted as necessary and reasonable.[14]

The New York Court of Appeals affirmed the decision without issuing an opinion.[15] Had the policeman, rather than the school official, searched the boy under the same circumstances, the evidence obtained probably would have been inadmissible in court. The search and seizure by the policeman might have been held illegal since "probable cause" had not been established. For the school official, only "reasonable suspicion" was required by the court.

In another case in a high school in Illinois, a student told the assistant principal that another student had a concealed gun on him. The assistant principal notified two policemen who had been assigned to the school. The officers accompanied the assistant principal to the classroom. The boy with the concealed weapon was brought into the hall. One of the officers ordered the boy not to move his hands and asked him if he had a gun. The boy said he did not. One officer held the boy's arms while the other removed a gun from his pants pocket.

In court, the boy was judged a delinquent for carrying a concealed gun. He appealed. He claimed that the police had improperly searched him. No probable cause for the search existed. Therefore, his lawyers argued, the search violated the boy's rights under the Fourth and Fourteenth Amendments. The evidence should have been suppressed.

The Supreme Court of Illinois in *In re Boykin* affirmed the decision of the lower court.[16] The Court held that the search by the police was reasonable and justified without a warrant or probable cause. The police could search the student immediately because they were acting on the request of the assistant principal.

In an Austin, Texas, high school, the dean received a tip that a student was in possession of marijuana. The dean reported this to the principal. The principal had the student brought to his office. The student was asked to empty his pockets. The boy was reluctant to do so. He complied, however, when the principal threatened to call the boy's father. When marijuana cigarettes were found, the principal called the boy's father and then the police. The boy was declared a delinquent in juvenile court. This decision was affirmed by the Texas Court of Civil Appeals in *Mercer* v. *State*.[17] The court held that the principal stood *in loco parentis*. Because of this, he acted as a private person, not as a governmental official. Therefore, the search was not covered by the Fourth Amendment. We will see in a later decision that this opinion is no longer held by any court.

School's Use of Sniff Dogs and Drug Detection

Federal courts have consistently held that a school district's use of trained dogs to sniff students' lockers and cars for drugs or alcohol does not violate the Fourth Amendment.[18]

In *Doe* v. *Renfrow* an Indiana school district conducted a search of all junior and senior high school students. Drug-sniffing dogs were used.[19] If the dog gave an "alert," the student was required to empty his or her pocket or purse. If the dog continued the "alert," the student would go to the nurse's office to be strip searched. A seventh grade girl was forced to undergo the strip search. No drugs were found on her. The drug dog's interest in her was probably caused by her own female dog, which she was in contact with that morning. The girl and her parents sued the school district for damages. The federal court held the school's actions reasonable. The Circuit Court of Appeals reversed. With regard to the strip search, it found:

> . . . that a nude search of a thirteen year old child is an invasion of constitutional rights of some magnitude.

A police officer is assisted by a drug-sniffing dog as he searches a vehicle for unlawful drugs.

More than that, it is a violation of any known principle of human decency.[20]

The Court held that the use of drug-sniffing dogs in schools did not violate the Fourth Amendment. An intrusive search of a young person, however, did. The United States Supreme Court refused to hear the case.[21]

Other federal and state courts are in disagreement as to whether a school's use of trained dogs to sniff students for the presence of drugs, without an individualized suspicion of the students searched, is a violation of the Fourth Amendment.[22] Only an eventual decision by the United States Supreme Court will settle the confusion surrounding this issue.

The use of metal detectors to search students at random for guns and weapons as they enter school has been held to be reasonable and justified by the governmental interest involved in student safety.[23]

Drug Testing in Schools

Most courts have held that testing of students' urine for traces of drugs, without reasonable suspicion by school districts, violates the Fourth Amendment.[24] However, drug testing as a precondition for student participation in sports was upheld by some courts.[25] This issue was finally resolved in 1995. The United States Supreme Court heard a school case on drug testing for student athletes in *Vernonia School District* v. *Acton*.[26]

School officials in an Oregon public school district observed an increase in discipline problems and drug use among students. Drug use increases the risk of injuries in sports. So school administrators met with parents to discuss a proposed drug testing policy for student athletes. With the unanimous

approval of the parents in attendance, the school
board enacted the testing program. All students
wishing to participate in interscholastic sports had to
sign a form, along with their parents, to have the
students' urine tested for drug traces. Athletes were
tested at the beginning of each sport season. Random
testing of 10 percent of the athletes was done weekly
during the season. In 1991 a seventh-grade student
and his parents refused to sign the testing consent
forms. Therefore, the school would not allow him to
participate in the football program.

The boy and his parents went to court. They
claimed that the school district's policy violated the
boy's constitutional rights. The federal district court
said that the drug testing policy was reasonable under
the circumstances. It dismissed the case. However, the
United States Court of Appeals reversed the decision.
It held that the school policy violated the Fourth
Amendment and a portion of the Oregon
Constitution.

On appeal, the United States Supreme Court
reversed the Court of Appeals. The Court found the
drug testing policy reasonable. It did not violate the
boy's rights under the Fourth Amendment.

Speaking for the Court, Justice Antonin Scalia
pointed out that the drug problems in the school
district, especially with students involved in
interscholastic athletics, were severe enough to take
action. Students, and in particular student athletes,
must have a decreased expectation of privacy in
school. The urine test is not a severe invasion of
privacy, and there was a demonstrated need for the
test.[27] Students may avoid the testing by choosing not
to participate in sports. The Court did not address the
issue of drug testing for all students.

The rule followed in this case is consistent with the practice followed at the time when the Fourth Amendment was enacted. The reasonableness of the search is determined by balancing the intrusion on the person's right of privacy against the interests of the government.

Landmark School Search Decision

Chapter 1 discussed *New Jersey* v. *T.L.O.* It was the first decision by the United States Supreme Court involving searching of a student in the public schools. Prior to this decision, some courts held that school officials conducting in-school searches of students were not governmental officials, but rather private parties. In this respect, they were acting *in loco parentis*. Therefore, they were not subject to the provisions of the Fourth Amendment.[28]

The majority of the states, however, held that school personnel were governmental officials. The Fourth Amendment did apply to student searches, but the special needs of the school situation call for a standard less exacting than probable cause.[29]

In Louisiana, state courts held that all school searches conducted required probable cause or a search warrant or they were considered unreasonable.[30] Courts throughout the United States were also divided over whether the exclusionary rule applied to Fourth Amendment violations by public school officials.

The Georgia courts have held that although the Fourth Amendment applies to the schools, the exclusionary rule does not.[31] Other courts have applied the exclusionary rule to exclude the material of unlawful school searches from criminal trials and delinquency proceedings.[32]

Byron White was appointed to the United States Supreme Court by President John F. Kennedy. He served as an Associate Justice from 1962 until 1993. He wrote the landmark school search and seizure decision in New Jersey v. T.L.O.

At this time, you might want to review the facts about *New Jersey* v. *T.L.O.*, found in Chapter 1 of this book. You will remember that the highest court in New Jersey had ruled that Mr. Choplick's search of T.L.O.'s purse had been unreasonable. Therefore, the New Jersey Supreme Court reversed the Appellate Court and suppressed the evidence that was found in the pocketbook.

In the appeal by the state of New Jersey to the United States Supreme Court, the sole issue of the appeal was whether or not the exclusionary rule should apply in an unlawful search and seizure by school officials.

In examining the entire case, the United States Supreme Court decided that:

1. The Fourth Amendment does apply to searches conducted by public school personnel and that they are considered governmental officials when they search students.

2. School personnel need not obtain a search warrant before searching a student under their control.

3. School officials may legally search a student on reasonable suspicion that the student is violating or has violated the law or school rules.

4. Even a limited bodily search of a student is a substantial invasion of privacy.

5. The legality of the search depends on all the circumstances of the search. Was the search justified at its inception and was it reasonably related in scope to the circumstances that justified the search in the first place?

In reversing the New Jersey Supreme Court's decision, the United States Supreme Court concluded that Mr. Choplick acted reasonably.[33] Both his initial search of T.L.O.'s purse to see if it contained cigarettes and his further, more thorough, search for marijuana were valid.

In its decision, the United States Supreme Court answered some questions relating to school searches and seizures. It neglected, however, to answer the question of whether the exclusionary rule applied in school search cases.[34] Since the Court found the searches reasonable, the rule was not applicable. Is a juvenile court case of this type considered a criminal case? Although the Court referred to the *Overton* decision, it did not rule on the legality of school locker and desk searches.[35] Most people believe that school locker and desk searches would be upheld by the Supreme Court. The Supreme Court offered no opinion on the question of searches conducted by school personnel in conjunction with police officers such as in *Boykin*.[36]

Schools have become more violent since the *T.L.O.* decision. In recent years, some public schools have used dogs to sniff out drugs. Some schools have even installed metal detectors to prevent students from bringing guns into the school.[37] The Supreme Court has never ruled on the legality of these practices. Some schools have resorted to testing students for drugs, with parents' consent when possible. In 1996 the National Parents' Resource Institute for Drug Education found that more than one in four high school seniors used illicit drugs once a month or more frequently during the school year.[38] In another national survey in 1996, 40 percent of high school seniors said they had used illegal drugs in the last year. Among high school tenth graders, it was 37.5 percent, and among eighth graders, it was 23.6 percent.[39] A Harris poll found that 22 percent of children in grades six through twelve "carried a weapon to school" in 1993.[40] A National Crime Survey revealed that nearly three million incidents of school crime occur in kindergarten through twelfth grade each year.[41]

There are still a number of problems to be addressed involving search and seizure in the schools. It is probable that the United States Supreme Court will agree to hear other school search cases involving one or more of these unanswered questions.

9

Looking Toward the Future

When the Fourth Amendment was ratified as part of the Bill of Rights in 1791, the Founding Fathers expected this amendment simply to protect American citizens from the kind of federal governmental search and seizures allowed by general warrants. Fourth Amendment rights were not considered as important as those rights protected by other amendments. Protection against unlawful search and seizure did not rank with freedoms of speech, religion, and the press. Nor, was it as important as the rights to freely assemble, to bear arms, or to have a speedy trial if accused of a crime.[1]

During the early years of our nation, the Fourth Amendment was a very specific protection that applied only to search and seizure intrusions by agents of the federal government. As the years passed, the United States Supreme Court modified its interpretation of the Fourth Amendment. Its scope was extended far beyond its original, limited purpose. The Supreme Court created a rule that any evidence that was seized in a manner not consistent with the Court's interpretation of what a search warrant should include could not be used in federal courts. Then this "exclusionary rule" was extended to the state courts in 1961. Cases involving Fourth Amendment violations increased dramatically.

As the population increased and society changed, so did the number of governmental searches. First, there were investigations of violations of liquor prohibition laws and later searches involved with illegal sales and use of drugs. Now, due to advanced technology, the legality of state and federal searches is even more frequently questioned. Aerial surveillance;

The Supreme Court in 1998. Front row, left to right: Antonin Scalia, John Paul Stevens, Chief Justice William H. Rehnquist, Sandra Day O'Connor, and Anthony M. Kennedy. Second row, left to right: Ruth Bader Ginsburg, David H. Souter, Clarence Thomas, and Stephen G. Breyer.

long-distance, high-resolution cameras; decoding devices; computer records; and communications on the Internet add to search possibilities.

Sixty percent of American households have cordless telephones. Their transmissions are easy to intercept with a simple store-bought transmitter. Since 1992 intercepting messages over cellular phones has been a federal crime. This law is almost impossible to enforce, however.

In addition, as the members of the Supreme Court change, so does the Court's interpretation of the Fourth Amendment. After over two hundred years,

"Oh, yeah! The decision of which judge is final?"

As this cartoon from The Wall Street Journal suggests, disagreements among Supreme Court Justices do occur.

what constitutes a legal search under the Fourth Amendment is unclear to many people, including judges. This is apparent, as evidenced by the number of reversals of state and federal court decisions by the United States Supreme Court. Even among the Supreme Court Justices, there is disagreement.

From the passage of the Bill of Rights in 1791 until the *Weeks* decision in 1914, fewer than a dozen cases involving the Fourth Amendment had been decided by the United States Supreme Court. Since then, the Supreme Court has issued almost four hundred decisions involving the Fourth Amendment.[2] The majority of these decisions have been by a divided court, a number by 5-to-4 decisions. There were also numerous Fourth Amendment cases that the Supreme Court refused to hear. In addition, there were certainly many more search and seizure cases held in state and federal courts that were never appealed to the United States Supreme Court.

In spite of all the questions about its application, the Fourth Amendment has become one of the primary protections for American citizens under the Bill of Rights. It guarantees privacy in our persons, homes, and communications, and protection against unwarranted search and seizure. When the government violates these rights, we can and should seek redress by the courts. When police officers perform lawful searches and seizures, and evidence is used to prosecute and punish accused criminals, the Fourth Amendment is working for all of us.

THE CONSTITUTION OF THE UNITED STATES

The text of the Constitution is presented here. All words are given their modern spelling and capitalization. Brackets [ ] indicate parts that have been changed or set aside by amendments.

Preamble

We the people of the United States, in order to form a more perfect Union, establish justice, insure domestic tranquility, provide for the common defense, promote the general welfare, and secure the blessings of liberty to ourselves and our posterity, do ordain and establish this Constitution for the United States of America.

ARTICLE I
The Legislative Branch

Section 1. All legislative powers herein granted shall be vested in a Congress of the United States, which shall consist of a Senate and House of Representatives.

The House of Representatives

Section 2. (1) The House of Representatives shall be composed of members chosen every second year by the people of the several states, and the electors in each state shall have the qualifications requisite for electors of the most numerous branch of the state legislature.

(2) No person shall be a representative who shall not have attained the age of twenty-five years, and been seven years a citizen of the United States, and who shall not, when elected, be an inhabitant of that state in which he shall be chosen.

(3) Representatives and direct taxes shall be apportioned among the several states which may be included within this Union, according to their respective numbers, [which shall be determined by adding to the whole number of free persons, including those bound to service for a term of years, and excluding Indians not taxed, three-fifths of all other persons]. The actual enumeration shall be made within three years after the first meeting of the Congress of the United States, and within every subsequent term of ten years, in such manner as they shall by law direct. The number of representatives shall not exceed one for every thirty thousand, but each state shall have at least one representative; [and until such enumeration shall be made, the state of New Hampshire shall be entitled to choose three, Massachusetts eight, Rhode Island and Providence Plantations one, Connecticut five, New York six, New Jersey four, Pennsylvania eight, Delaware one, Maryland six, Virginia ten, North Carolina five, South Carolina five, and Georgia three].

(4) When vacancies happen in the representation from any state, the executive authority thereof shall issue writs of election to fill such vacancies.

(5) The House of Representatives shall choose their Speaker and other officers; and shall have the sole power of impeachment.

The Senate

Section 3. (1) The Senate of the United States shall be composed of two senators from each state, [chosen by the legislature thereof,] for six years; and each senator shall have one vote.

(2) Immediately after they shall be assembled in consequence of the first election, they shall be divided as equally as may be into three classes. The seats of the senators of the first class shall be vacated at the expiration of the second year, of the second class at the expiration of the fourth year, and of the third class at the expiration of the sixth year, so that one-third may be chosen every second year; [and if vacancies happen by resignation, or otherwise, during the recess of the legislature of any state, the executive thereof may make temporary appointments until the next meeting of the legislature, which shall then fill such vacancies].

(3) No person shall be a senator who shall not have attained to the age of thirty years, and been nine years a citizen of the United States, and who shall not, when elected, be an inhabitant of that state for which he shall be chosen.

(4) The Vice President of the United States shall be president of the Senate, but shall have no vote, unless they be equally divided.

(5) The Senate shall choose their other officers, and also a president *pro tempore*, in the absence of the Vice President, or when he shall exercise the office of President of the United States.

(6) The Senate shall have the sole power to try all impeachments. When sitting for that purpose, they shall be on oath or affirmation. When the President of the United States is tried, the Chief Justice shall preside: and no person shall be convicted without the concurrence of two-thirds of the members present.

(7) Judgement in cases of impeachment shall not extend further than to removal from office, and disqualification to hold and enjoy any office of honor, trust, or profit under the United States: but the party convicted shall nevertheless be liable and subject to indictment, trial, judgement and punishment, according to law.

Organization of Congress

Section 4. (1) The times, places and manner of holding elections for senators and representatives, shall be prescribed in each state by the legislature thereof; but the Congress may at any time by law make or alter such regulations, [except as to the places of choosing senators].

(2) The Congress shall assemble at least once in every year, [and such meeting shall be on the first Monday in December], unless they shall by law appoint a different day.

Section 5. (1) Each house shall be the judge of the elections, returns and qualifications of its own members, and a majority of each shall constitute a quorum to do business; but a smaller number may adjourn from day to day, and may be authorized to compel the attendance of absent members, in such manner, and under such penalties as each house may provide.

(2) Each house may determine the rules of its proceedings, punish its members for disorderly behavior, and, with the concurrence of two-thirds, expel a member.

(3) Each house shall keep a journal of its proceedings, and from time to time publish the same, excepting such parts as may in their judgement require secrecy; and the yeas and nays of the members of either house on any question shall, at the desire of one-fifth of those present, be entered on the journal.

(4) Neither house, during the session of Congress, shall, without the consent of the other, adjourn for more than three days, nor to any other place than that in which the two houses shall be sitting.

Section 6. (1) The senators and representatives shall receive a compensation for their services, to be ascertained by law, and paid out of the treasury of the United States. They shall in all cases, except treason, felony and breach of the peace, be privileged from arrest during their attendance at the session of their respective houses, and in going to and returning from the same; and for any speech or debate in either house, they shall not be questioned in any other place.

(2) No senator or representative shall, during the time for which he was elected, be appointed to any civil office under the authority of the United States, which shall have been created, or the emoluments whereof shall have been increased during such time; and no person holding any office under the United States shall be a member of either house during his continuance in office.

Section 7. (1) All bills for raising revenue shall originate in the House of Representatives; but the Senate may propose or concur with amendments as on other bills.

(2) Every bill which shall have passed the House of Representatives and the Senate, shall, before it become a law, be presented to the President of the United States; if he approve he shall sign it, but if not he shall return it, with his objections to that house in which it shall have originated, who shall enter the objections at large on their journal, and proceed to reconsider it. If after such reconsideration two-thirds of that house shall agree to pass the bill, it shall be sent, together with the objections, to the other house, by which it shall likewise be reconsidered, and if approved by two-thirds of that house, it shall become a law. But in all such cases the votes of both houses shall be determined by yeas and nays, and the names of the persons voting for and against the bill shall be entered on the journal of each house respectively. If any bill shall not be returned by the President within ten days (Sundays excepted) after it shall have been presented to him, the same shall be a law, in like manner as if he had signed it, unless the Congress by their

adjournment prevent its return, in which case it shall not be a law.

(3) Every order, resolution, or vote to which the concurrence of the Senate and House of Representatives may be necessary (except on a question of adjournment) shall be presented to the President of the United States; and before the same shall take effect, shall be approved by him, or being disapproved by him, shall be repassed by two-thirds of the Senate and House of Representatives, according to the rules and limitations prescribed in the case of a bill.

Powers Granted to Congress

The Congress shall have power:

Section 8. (1) To lay and collect taxes, duties, imposts and excises, to pay the debts and provide for the common defense and general welfare of the United States; but all duties, imposts and excises shall be uniform throughout the United States;

(2) To borrow money on the credit of the United States;

(3) To regulate commerce with foreign nations, and among the several states, and with the Indian tribes;

(4) To establish an uniform rule of naturalization, and uniform laws on the subject of bankruptcies throughout the United States;

(5) To coin money, regulate the value thereof, and of foreign coin, and fix the standard of weights and measures;

(6) To provide for the punishment of counterfeiting the securities and current coin of the United States;

(7) To establish post offices and post roads;

(8) To promote the progress of science and useful arts, by securing for limited times to authors and inventors the exclusive right to their respective writings and discoveries;

(9) To constitute tribunals inferior to the Supreme Court;

(10) To define and punish piracies and felonies committed on the high seas, and offenses against the law of nations;

(11) To declare war, grant letters of marque and reprisal, and make rules concerning captures on land and water;

(12) To raise and support armies, but no appropriation of money to that use shall be for a longer term than two years;

(13) To provide and maintain a navy;

(14) To make rules for the government and regulation of the land and naval forces;

(15) To provide for calling forth the militia to execute the laws of the Union, suppress insurrections and repel invasions;

(16) To provide for organizing, arming, and disciplining the militia, and for governing such part of them as may be employed in the service of the United States, reserving to the states respectively, the appointment of the officers, and the authority of training the militia according to the discipline prescribed by Congress;

(17) To exercise exclusive legislation in all cases whatsoever, over such district (not exceeding ten miles square) as may, by cession of particular states, and the acceptance of Congress, become the seat of the government of the United States, and to exercise like authority over all places purchased by the consent of the legislature of the state in which the same shall be, for the erection of forts, magazines, arsenals, dockyards, and other needful buildings;—And

(18) To make all laws which shall be necessary and proper for carrying into execution the foregoing powers, and all other powers vested by this Constitution in the government of the United States, or in any department or officer thereof.

Powers Forbidden to Congress

Section 9. (1) The migration or importation of such persons as any of the states now existing shall think proper to admit, shall not be prohibited by the Congress prior to the year one thousand eight hundred and eight, but a tax or duty may be imposed on such importation, not exceeding ten dollars for each person.

(2) The privilege of the writ of *habeas corpus* shall not be suspended, unless when in cases of rebellion or invasion the public safety may require it.

(3) No bill of attainder or *ex post facto* law shall be passed.

(4) No capitation, [or other direct,] tax shall be laid, unless in proportion to the census or enumeration herein before directed to be taken.

(5) No tax or duty shall be laid on articles exported from any state.

(6) No preference shall be given by any regulation of commerce or revenue to the ports of one state over those of another: nor shall vessels bound to, or from, one state, be obliged to enter, clear, or pay duties in another.

(7) No money shall be drawn from the treasury, but in consequence of appropriations made by law; and a regular statement and account of the receipts and expenditures of all public money shall be published from time to time.

(8) No title of nobility shall be granted by the United States: And no person holding any office or profit or trust under them, shall, without the consent of the Congress, accept of any present, emolument, office, or title, of any kind whatsoever, from any king, prince, or foreign state.

Powers Forbidden to the States

Section 10. (1) No state shall enter into any treaty, alliance, or confederation; grant letters of marque and reprisal; coin money; emit bills of credit; make any thing but gold and silver coin a tender in payment of debts; pass any bill of attainder, *ex post facto* law, or law impairing the obligation of contracts, or grant any title of nobility.

(2) No state shall, without the consent of the Congress, lay any imposts or duties on imports or exports, except what may be absolutely necessary for executing its inspection laws: and the net produce of all duties and imposts, laid by any state on imports or exports, shall be for the use of the treasury of the United States, and all such laws shall be subject to the revision and control of the Congress.

(3) No state shall, without the consent of Congress, lay any duty of tonnage, keep troops, or ships of war in time of peace, enter into any agreement or compact with another state, or with a foreign power, or engage in war, unless actually invaded, or in such imminent danger as will not admit of delay.

Article II
The Executive Branch

Section 1. (1) The executive power shall be vested in a President of the United States of America. He shall hold his office during the term of four years, and, together with the Vice President, chosen for the same term, be elected as follows:

(2) Each state shall appoint, in such manner as the legislature thereof may direct, a number of electors, equal to the whole number of senators and representatives to which the state may be entitled in the Congress: but no senator or representative, or person holding an office of trust or profit under the United States, shall be appointed an elector.

(3) [The electors shall meet in their respective states, and vote by ballot for two persons, of whom one at least shall not be an inhabitant of the same state with themselves. And they shall make a list of all the persons voted for, and of the number of votes for each; which list they shall sign and certify, and transmit sealed to the seat of government of the United States, directed to the president of the Senate. The president of the Senate shall, in the presence of the Senate and House of Representatives, open all the certificates, and the votes shall then be counted. The person having the greatest number of votes shall be the President, if such number be a majority of the whole number of electors appointed; and if there be more than one who have such majority, and have an equal number of votes, then the House of Representatives shall immediately choose by ballot one of them for President; and if no person have a majority, then from the five highest on the list the said House shall in like manner choose the President. But in choosing the President, the votes shall be taken by states, the representation from each state having one vote; a quorum for this purpose shall consist of a member or members from two-thirds of the states, and a majority of all the states shall be necessary to a choice. In every case, after the choice of the President, the person having the greatest number of votes of the electors shall be the Vice President. But if there should remain two or more who have equal votes, the Senate shall choose from them by ballot the Vice President.]

(4) The Congress may determine the time of choosing the electors, and the day on which they shall give their votes; which day shall be the same throughout the United States.

(5) No person except a natural-born citizen, or a citizen of the United States, at the time of the adoption of this Constitution, shall be eligible to the office of President; neither shall any person be eligible to that office who shall not have attained to the age of thirty-five years, and been fourteen years a resident within the United States.

(6) In case of the removal of the President from office, or of his death, resignation, or inability to discharge the powers and duties of the said office, the same shall devolve on the Vice President, and the Congress may by law provide for the case of removal, death, resignation, or inability, both of the President and Vice President, declaring what officer shall then act as President, and such officer shall act accordingly, until the disability be removed, or a President shall be elected.

(7) The President shall, at stated times, receive for his services, a compensation, which shall neither be increased nor diminished during the period for which he shall have been elected, and he shall not receive within that period any other emolument from the United States, or any of them.

(8) Before he enter on the execution of his office, he shall take the following oath or affirmation: "I do solemnly swear (or affirm) that I will faithfully execute the office of the President of the United States, and will to the best of my ability, preserve, protect and defend the Constitution of the United States."

Section 2. (1) The President shall be commander-in-chief of the Army and Navy of the United States, and of the militia of the several states, when called into the actual service of the United States; he may require the opinion, in writing, of the principal officer in each of the executive departments, upon any subject relating to the duties of their respective offices, and he shall have power to grant reprieves and pardons for offenses against the United States, except in cases of impeachment.

(2) He shall have power, by and with the advice and consent of the Senate, to make treaties, provided two-thirds of the senators present concur; and he shall nominate, and by and with the advice and consent of the Senate, shall appoint ambassadors, other public ministers and consuls, judges of the Supreme Court, and all other officers of the United States, whose appointments are not herein otherwise provided for, and which shall be established by law: but the Congress may by law vest the appointment of such inferior officers, as they think proper, in the President alone, in the courts of law, or in the heads of departments.

(3) The President shall have the power to fill up all vacancies that may happen during the recess of the Senate, by granting commissions which shall expire at the end of their next session.

Section 3. He shall from time to time give to the Congress information of the state of the Union, and recommend to their consideration such measures as he shall judge necessary and expedient; he may, on extraordinary occasions, convene both houses, or either of them, and in case of disagreement between them, with respect to the time of adjournment, he may adjourn them to such time as he shall think proper; he shall receive ambassadors and other public ministers; he shall take care that the laws be faithfully executed, and shall commission all the officers of the United States.

Section 4. The President, Vice President and all civil officers of the United States, shall be removed from office on impeachment for, and conviction of, treason, bribery, or other high crimes and misdemeanors.

ARTICLE III
The Judicial Branch

Section 1. The judicial power of the United States, shall be vested in one Supreme Court, and in such inferior courts as the Congress may from time to time ordain and establish. The judges, both of the Supreme and inferior courts, shall hold their offices during good behaviour, and shall, at stated times, receive for their services, a compensation, which shall not be diminished during their continuance in office.

Section 2. (1) The judicial power shall extend to all cases, in law and equity, arising under this Constitution, the laws of the United States, and treaties made, or which shall be made, under their authority; —to all cases affecting ambassadors, other public ministers and consuls;—to all cases of admiralty and maritime jurisdiction;—to controversies to which the United States shall be a party;—to controversies between two or more states, [between a state and citizens of another state;], between citizens of different states;—between citizens of the same state claiming lands under grants of different states, and between a state, or the citizens thereof, and foreign states, [citizens or subjects].

(2) In all cases affecting ambassadors, other public ministers and consuls, and those in which a state shall be party, the Supreme Court shall have original jurisdiction. In all the other cases before mentioned, the Supreme Court shall have appellate jurisdiction, both as to law and fact, with such exceptions, and under such regulations as the Congress shall make.

(3) The trial of all crimes, except in cases of impeachment, shall be by jury; and such trial shall be held in the state where the said crimes shall have been committed; but when not committed within any state, the trial shall be at such place or places as the Congress may by law have directed.

Section 3. (1) Treason against the United States, shall consist only in levying war against them, or in adhering to their enemies, giving them aid and comfort. No person shall be convicted of treason unless on the testimony of two witnesses to the same overt act, or on confession in open court.

(2) The Congress shall have power to declare the punishment of treason, but no attainder of treason shall work corruption of blood, or forfeiture, except during the life of the person attainted.

ARTICLE IV
Relation of the States to Each Other
Section 1. Full faith and credit shall be given in each state to the public acts, records, and judicial

proceedings of every other state. And the Congress may by general laws prescribe the manner in which such acts, records and proceedings shall be proved, and the effect thereof.

Section 2. (1) The citizens of each state shall be entitled to all privileges and immunities of citizens in the several states.

(2) A person charged in any state with treason, felony, or other crime, who shall flee justice, and be found in another state, shall on demand of the executive authority of the state from which he fled, be delivered up, to be removed to the state having jurisdiction of the crime.

(3) [No person held to service or labor in one state, under the laws thereof, escaping into another, shall, in consequence of any law or regulation therein, be discharged from such service or labor, but shall be delivered up on claim of the party to whom such service or labor may be due.]

Federal-State Relations

Section 3. (1) New states may be admitted by the Congress into this Union; but no new state shall be formed or erected within the jurisdiction of any other state, nor any state be formed by the junction of two or more states, without the consent of the legislatures of the states concerned as well as of the Congress.

(2) The Congress shall have power to dispose of and make all needful rules and regulations respecting the territory or other property belonging to the United States; and nothing in this Constitution shall be so construed as to prejudice any claims of the United States, or of any particular state.

Section 4. The United States shall guarantee to every state in this Union a republican form of government, and shall protect each of them against invasion; and on application of the legislature, or of the executive (when the legislature cannot be convened), against domestic violence.

ARTICLE V
Amending the Constitution

The Congress, whenever two-thirds of both houses shall deem it necessary, shall propose amendments to this Constitution, or, on the application of the legislatures of two-thirds of the several states, shall call a convention for proposing amendments, which, in either case, shall be valid to all intents and purposes, as part of this Constitution, when ratified by the legislatures of three-fourths of the several states, or by conventions in three-fourths thereof, as the one or the other mode of ratification may be proposed by the Congress; provided [that no amendment which may be made prior to the year one thousand eight hundred and eight, shall in any manner affect the first and fourth clauses in the ninth section of the first article; and] that no state, without its consent, shall be deprived of its equal suffrage in the Senate.

ARTICLE VI
National Debts

(1) All debts contracted and engagements entered into, before the adoption of this Constitution, shall be as

valid against the United States under this Constitution, as under the Confederation.

Supremacy of the National Government

(2) This Constitution, and the laws of the United States which shall be made in pursuance thereof; and all treaties made, or which shall be made, under the authority of the United States shall be the supreme law of the land; and the judges in every state shall be bound thereby, any thing in the constitution or laws of any state to the contrary notwithstanding.

(3) The senators and representatives before mentioned, and the members of the several state legislatures, and all executive and judicial officers, both of the United States and of the several states, shall be bound by oath or affirmation, to support this Constitution; but no religious test shall ever be required as a qualification to any office or public trust under the United States.

ARTICLE VII
Ratifying the Constitution

The ratification of the conventions of nine states, shall be sufficient for the establishment of this Constitution between the states so ratifying the same.

Done in convention by the unanimous consent of the states present the seventeenth day of September in the year of our Lord one thousand seven hundred and eighty-seven and of the independence of the United States of America the twelfth. In witness whereof we have hereunto subscribed our names.

Amendments to the Constitution

The first ten amendments, known as the Bill of Rights, were proposed on September 25, 1789. They were ratified, or accepted, on December 15, 1791. They were adopted because some states refused to approve the Constitution unless a Bill of Rights, protecting individuals from various unjust acts of government, was added.

Amendment 1

Freedom of religion, speech, and the press;
rights of assembly and petition

Amendment 2

Right to bear arms

Amendment 3

Housing of soldiers

Amendment 4

Search and arrest warrants

Amendment 5

Rights in criminal cases

Amendment 6

Rights to a fair trial

Amendment 7

Rights in civil cases

Amendment 8

Bails, fines, and punishments

Amendment 9

Rights retained by the people

Amendment 10

Powers retained by the states and the people

Amendment 11

Lawsuits against states

Amendment 12

Election of the President and Vice President

Amendment 13

Abolition of slavery

Amendment 14

Civil rights

Amendment 15

African-American suffrage

Amendment 16

Income taxes

Amendment 17

Direct election of senators

Amendment 18

Prohibition of liquor

Amendment 19

Women's suffrage

Amendment 20

Terms of the President and Congress

Amendment 21

Repeal of prohibition

Amendment 22

Presidential term limits

Amendment 23

Suffrage in the District of Columbia

Amendment 24

Poll taxes

Amendment 25

Presidential disability and succession

Amendment 26

Suffrage for eighteen-year-olds

Amendment 27

Congressional salaries

Chapter Notes

Chapter 1

1. United States Constitution, Amendment IV.
2. *T.L.O.* v. *Piscataway Bd. of Ed.* No. C2865-79 (N.J. Super. Ct. Ch Div, March 31, 1980).
3. *State ex rel T.L.O.*, 178 N.J. Super. 329, 428 A.2d 1327 (1980).
4. *State ex rel T.L.O.*, 185 N.J. Super. 279, 448 A.2d 493 (1982).
5. *State ex rel T.L.O.*, 94 N.J. 331, 463 A.2d 934 (1983).
6. *New Jersey* v. *T.L.O.*, 464 U.S. 991 (1983).
7. *New Jersey* v. *T.L.O.*, 469 U.S. 325 (1985).

Chapter 2

1. United States Constitution, Amendment IV.
2. Nelson B. Lasson, *The History and Development of the Fourth Amendment to the United States Constitution* (Baltimore, Md.: The Johns Hopkins Press, 1937), pp. 26–29.
3. Ibid., p. 31.
4. Ibid., p. 35; See *Boyd* v. *United States*, 116 U.S. 616, 630 (1886).
5. *Entick* v. *Carrington*, 95 Eng.Rep.807 (1765).
6. Ibid., p. 1063.
7. Lasson, p. 47.
8. Paula A. Franklin, *The Fourth Amendment* (Englewood Cliffs, N.J.: Silver Burdett Press, Inc., 1991), p. 32.
9. Lasson, p. 51.
10. Diane Ravitch, ed., *The American Reader—Words that Moved a Nation* (New York: Harper Collins, 1990), p. 11.
11. Lasson, p. 59.
12. Charles A. Reynard, *Freedom from Unreasonable Search and Seizure—A Second Class Constitutional Right? Indiana Law Journal*, Volume 25, No. 3, Spring 1950, p. 272.

Chapter 3

1. Albert Marrin, *The War for Independence, The Story of the American Revolution* (New York: Atheneum, Macmillan Publishing Company, 1988), pp. 43–46.
2. The Declaration of Independence, July 4, 1776.

3. Donald Barr Chidsey, *The Birth of the Constitution* (New York: Crown Publishers, 1966), p. 23; Denis J. Hauptly, *A Convention of Delegates—The Creation of the Constitution* (New York: Atheneum, 1987), pp. 21–22.

4. Donald A. Ritchie, *The U.S. Constitution* (New York: Chelsea House Publishers, 1989), p. 31.

5. Max Farrand, ed., *The Records of the Federal Convention of 1789, Vol. 2* (New Haven, Conn.: Yale University Press, 1937), p. 588; Catherine Drinker Bowen, *Miracle at Philadelphia* (Boston: Little Brown and Company, 1966), p. 263.

6. Edmund Lindop, *Birth of the Constitution* (Hillside, N.J.: Enslow Publishers, Inc., 1987), p. 71; Herbert M. Atherton and J. Jackson Barlow, *The Bill of Rights and Beyond* (Washington, D.C.: Commission on the Bicentennial of the United States, Government Printing Office, 1991), p. 33.

7. Linda Carlson Johnson, *Our Constitution* (Brookfield, Conn.: The Millbrook Press, 1992), p. 28.

8. Arval A. Morris, *The Constitution and American Education* (St. Paul, Minn.: West Publishing Company, 1974), p. 34.

9. Annals of Congress, 1st Congress, 1st Session, p. 783; Reynard, p. 275.

10. Ibid., pp. 275–276.

11. Edward Dumbauld, *The Bill of Rights and What It Means Today* (Tulsa, Okla.: University of Oklahoma Press, 1957), pp. 40–44.

12. Ibid., p. 50.

13. Reynard, p. 276.

Chapter 4

1. United States Constitution, Article III, Section 1 and Section 2.

2. Bernard Schwartz, *A History of the Supreme Court* (New York: Oxford University Press, Inc., 1993), pp. 16, 383.

3. *Ex parte Burford*, 7 U.S. 448 (1806).

4. Ibid., pp. 450–451.

5. Ibid., pp. 451–453.

6. *Locke v. United States*, 11 U.S. 339 (1813).

7. 47 Am J1st Search, Para. 22, Taken from *Brinegar v. United States*, 338 U.S. 160 (1949).

8. *Smith v. Maryland*, 59 U.S. 71 (1855).

9. Ibid., p. 76.

10. *Murray's Lessee v. Hoboken Land and Improvement Company*, 59 U.S. 272 (1855).

11. *Ex parte Jackson*, 96 U.S. 727 (1877).

12. Ibid.

13. *Boyd* v. *United States,* 116 U.S. 616, (1886).

14. Ibid., p. 622.

15. Ibid., p. 630.

16. Ibid., p. 638.

Chapter 5

1. Nelson B. Lasson, *The History and Development of the Fourth Amendment to the United States Constitution* (New York: The John Hopkins Press, 1937), p. 106.

2. *Weeks* v. *United States,* 232 U.S. 383 (1914).

3. Ibid., p. 393.

4. *Wolf* v. *Colorado,* 338 U.S. 25, 35–36 (1949).

5. *Weeks,* p. 392.

6. *Gouled* v. *United States,* 255 U.S. 298 (1921).

7. *Burdeau* v. *McDowell,* 256 U.S. 465 (1921).

8. *United States* v. *Jacobsen,* 466 U.S. 109 (1984).

9. *Carroll* v. *United States,* 267 U.S. 132 (1925).

10. Ibid., pp. 160–161.

11. Ibid., p. 161, citing *Lock* v. *United States,* 11 U.S. 339 (1813).

12. *Byars* v. *United States,* 273 U.S. 28 (1927).

13. Ibid., p. 32.

14. *United States* v. *Lee,* 274 U.S. 559 (1927).

15. Ibid., p. 563.

Chapter 6

1. *Wolf* v. *Colorado,* 338 U.S. 25 (1949).

2. *Rea* v. *United States,* 350 U.S. 214 (1956).

3. *Elkins* v. *United States,* 364 U.S. 206 (1960).

4. Ibid., pp. 223–224.

5. *Mapp* v. *Ohio,* 367 U.S. 643 (1961).

6. Ibid., pp. 671–672.

7. *Aguilar* v. *Texas,* 378 U.S. 108 (1964); *Spinelli* v. *United States,* 393 U.S. 410 (1969).

8. *Spinelli* at p. 429.

9. *Coolidge* v. *New Hampshire,* 403 U.S. 443 (1971).

10. *Marcus* v. *Search Warrants of Property at 104 East Tenth Street, Kansas City, Missouri,* 367 U.S. 717 (1961); *Wong Sun* v. *United States,* 371 U.S. 471 (1963); *Fahy* v. *Connecticut* 375 U.S. 5 (1963); *Preston* v. *United States,* 376 U.S. 364 (1964).

11. *Bivens* v. *Six Unknown Named Agents of Federal Bureau of Narcotics,* 403 U.S. 388, 416 (1971).

12. Ibid., p. 418.

13. *Illinois* v. *Gates,* 462 U.S. 213 (1983).

14. *Nix* v. *Williams*, 467 U.S. 431 (1984).

15. *United States* v. *Leon*, 468 U.S. 897 (1984).

16. *Massachusetts* v. *Sheppard*, 468 U.S. 981 (1984).

17. *Terry* v. *Ohio*, 392 U.S. 1 (1968).

18. Ibid., pp. 30–31.

19. *Sibron* v. *New York*, 392 U.S. 40 (1968).

20. *California* v. *Hodari D.*, 499 U.S. 621 (1991).

21. *Bivens*, 403 U.S. 388 (1971).

22. *Anderson* v. *Creighton*, 483 U.S. 635 (1987).

Chapter 7

1. *Olmstead* v. *United States*, 277 U.S. 438 (1928).

2. Ibid., pp. 464–465.

3. *Goldman* v. *United States*, 316 U.S. 129 (1942).

4. *Katz* v. *United States*, 369 F2d 130.

5. *Katz* v. *United States*, 389 U.S. 347 (1967).

6. Ibid., p. 359.

7. Ibid. pp. 360–361.

8. *Hester* v. *United States*, 265 U.S. 57 (1924).

9. *Oliver* v. *United States*, 466 U.S. 170 (1984).

10. Ibid., p. 181.

11. *California* v. *Ciraolo*, 476 U.S. 207 (1986).

12. Ibid., p. 216.

13. *Florida* v. *Riley*, 488 U.S. 445; 102 L.Ed.2d 835 (1989).

14. Ibid., p. 842.

15. *United States* v. *Edwards*, 498 F.2d 496 (1974).

16. Ibid., p. 500.

17. *Reid* v. *Georgia*, 448 U.S. 438 (1980).

18. *United States* v. *Sokolow*, 490 U.S. 1 (1989).

19. *Rochin* v. *California*, 342 U.S. 165 (1952).

20. Ibid., p. 172.

21. *Schmerber* v. *California*, 384 U.S. 757 (1966).

22. *Cupp* v. *Murphy*, 412 U.S. 291 (1973).

23. *Winston* v. *Lee*, 470 U.S. 753 (1985).

24. *Skinner* v. *Railway Labor Executives' Association*, 489 U.S. 602 (1989).

25. *National Treasury Employees Union* v. *Von Raab*, 489 U.S. 656 (1989).

26. *Chandler* v. *Miller*, 73 F.3d 1543 (11th Cir. 1996).

27. *Chandler* v. *Miller*, 520 U.S. 137 L.Ed.2d 513 (1997).

Chapter 8

1. *People* v. *Overton*, 20 N.Y.2d 360 (1967).

2. Ibid., pp. 362–363.

3. *Overton* v. *New York*, 393 U.S. 85 (1968).

4. *Bumper v. North Carolina,* 391 U.S. 543 (1968).

5. 24 N.Y.2d 522 (1969).

6. *Overton v. Rieger,* 401 U.S. 1003 (1971).

7. *State v. Stein,* 456 P.2d 1 (Kan. 1969).

8. Ibid., p. 3.

9. *Miranda v. Arizona,* 384 U.S. 436 (1966).

10. *Stein v. Kansas,* 397 U.S. 947 (1970).

11. *In re Donaldson,* 75 Cal. Rptr. 220 (Ct. App. 1969).

12. See *Christofides v. Hellenic Orthodox Church,* 227 N.Y.S.2d 946 (1962).

13. *People v. Jackson,* 319 N.Y.S.2d 731 (App. Div. 1971).

14. Ibid., p. 736.

15. 30 N.Y.2d 734 (1972).

16. *In re Boykin,* 39 Ill.2d 617, 237 N.E.2d 460 (1968).

17. *Mercer v. State,* 450 S.W.2d 715 (Tex. 1970).

18. *Zamora v. Pomeroy,* 639 F.2d 662 (10th Cir. 1981).

19. *Doe v. Renfrow,* 631 F.2d 91 (7th Cir. 1980).

20. Ibid., p. 643.

21. *Doe v. Renfrow,* 451 U.S. 1022 (1981).

22. *Horton v. Goose Creek Independent School District,* 690 F.2d 470 (1982).

23. *People v. Dukes,* 580 N.Y.S.2d 850 (Criminal Court, 1992).

24. *Anable v. Ford,* 663 F.Supp. 149 (1987).

25. *Schaill by Kross v. Tippecanoe School Corp.,* 864 F.2d 1309 (7th Cir. 1988); *Brooks v. East Chambers School District,* 730 F.Supp. 759 (Tex. 1989).

26. *Vernonia School District v. Acton,* 515 U.S.; 132 L.Ed.2d 564 (1995).

27. Ibid., p. 579.

28. See *D.R.C. v. State,* 646 P2d 252 (Alaska App. 1982); *In re G.,* 11 Cal. App.3rd 1193 (1970); *R.C.M. v. State,* 660 SW2d 552 (Tex. App. 1983).

29. *Bilbrey v. Brown,* 738 F2d 1462 (CA9 1884); *Horton v. Goose Creek Independent School Dist.,* 690 F2d (CA5 1982); *State v. Baccino,* 282 A2d 869 (Del Super 1971).

30. See *State v. Mora,* 307 So.2d 317 (La.) vacated, 423 U.S. 809 (1975), on remand, 330 So.2d 900 (La. 1976); others have held that the probable cause standard is applicable where police are involved in a search, see *M. V. Board of Ed. Ball-Chatham Community Unit School Dist. No. 5,* 429 F.Supp. 288 (SD Ill. 1977); or where the search is highly intrusive, see *M.M. v. Anker,* 607 F.2d 588 (CA2 1979).

31. *State v. Lamb,* 137 Ga.App.437, 224 SE2d 51 (1976).

32. *People* v. *Scott D.*, 34 N.Y. 483 (1974); *State ex rel T.L.O.*, 94 N.J. 331 (1983).

33. *New Jersey* v. *T.L.O.*, 469 U.S. 325, p. 327.

34. Ibid., p. 334.

35. Ibid., p. 338.

36. Ibid., p. 342.

37. Opinion of the Attorney General, State of California, No. 92–201 (October 1992).

38. *The New York Times*, "Schools Administrators Test for Drugs and Alcohol," February 9, 1997, p. 14.

39. *The New York Times*, "Adolescent Drug Use Continues to Rise," December 20, 1996, p. B12.

40. Lawrence F. Rossow, "Refining the 'Expelled' Fourth Amendment and T.L.O. for Realistic Schools", *Journal of Law & Education*, Vol. 24, No. 1, Winter 1995, pp. 85–89.

41. Ibid., p. 85.

Chapter 9

1. Charles A. Reynard, "Freedom From Unreasonable Search and Seizure—A Second Class Constitutional Right?" *Indiana Law Journal*, Volume 25, Number 3, Spring 1950, p. 259.

2. William W. Greenhalgh, *The Fourth Amendment Handbook, A Chronological Survey of Supreme Court Decisions* (Chicago: American Bar Association Publications, 1995), p. 21–102.

Glossary

amendment—A new provision to the United States Constitution, changing a particular portion of the Constitution.

appeal—A request to a higher court to review the decision of a lower court.

automobile exception—A search warrant requirement, under the Fourth Amendment, is not necessary when a law enforcement officer has probable cause to search an automobile.

certiorari—Latin term meaning "to be informed of." An order to review a lower court's decision. When the Supreme Court agrees to hear a case from a lower court, it grants *certiorari*. When the Supreme Court refuses to hear a case from a lower court, it denies *certiorari* and the decision of the lower court remains.

civil case—A legal action in which one person sues another person to recover damages for a wrong done to him or her.

classified material—Documents that have been designated secret or confidential.

common law—Law based on tradition and following the rule of previous court decisions.

concurring opinion—The opinion of a judge who agrees with the majority in a court decision, but his or her reasons for the decision are different from the majority.

criminal case—A legal action in which the state or federal government initiates legal action against a person for a crime he or she has committed.

customs—Taxes or duties imposed by the government on goods brought into a country.

dissenting opinion—The opinion of a judge who disagrees with the majority in a court decision.

exclusionary rule—A United States Supreme Court determination that any evidence that is obtained illegally may not be used in a criminal trial.

general warrant—A legal document in early England that allowed government agents to search and seize any person, home, or business.

habeas corpus—Latin term meaning "you have the body." An appeal to a court that a person is being held or confined in jail without sufficient cause.

indictment—A formal accusation or charge that a person has committed a crime.

in loco parentis—Latin phrase meaning "in place of the parent." The term used for a person who takes on some of the rights and responsibilities of the parent, such as a school official.

landmark decision—A reported case of great importance because it sets a precedent that other courts follow in later, similar cases.

majority opinion—The opinion of more than half of the Justices on the court.

mere evidence rule—A Supreme Court ruling that a valid warrant may not be issued for a search of private papers and materials that are not illegal in themselves, but simply are to be used as evidence by a government prosecutor.

Miranda warning—An individual held in custody for interrogation by a law enforcement officer must be warned of the constitutional right to remain silent, that any statement made may be used as evidence, and the right to the presence of an attorney.

nonresident alien—A person who is neither a citizen nor a resident of the United States.

plain view exception—Search warrant requirement under the Fourth Amendment is not necessary when a police officer, if lawfully in a premise, sees something that is incriminating.

precedent—A court decision that is followed by other courts.

probable cause—A reasonable ground for suspicion supported by circumstances that would make a cautious person believe that the person accused has committed the offense of which he or she is suspected.

qualified immunity—An exemption from civil liability for a federal officer in the performance of his job in good faith.

ratification—The formal sanction or approval of something.

reasonable suspicion—The existence of a reasonable belief that the accused is guilty, but less than probable cause.

remand—To return a case to a lower court by appellate court for further consideration.

sovereign—Independent of all other authority.

stop and frisk—Supreme Court rule allowing a police officer to stop a suspect to investigate the situation upon reasonable suspicion that a crime has been committed or is about to be committed. An officer may pat down a suspect to see if that person is armed. The officer does not need probable cause.

summary judgment—A judgment granted by a court to a person without the necessity of a trial. A motion for summary judgement may be made when all the facts are known by the judge.

suppress evidence—To keep certain evidence from being used in court.

vacate—To set aside or void the judgment of a lower court.

valid warrant—A warrant based on probable cause that meets the requirements of the Fourth Amendment.

writ of assistance—In colonial times, this document allowed government agents to search a person's home or place of business for an unlimited time.

Further Reading

Atherton, Herbert M., and J. Jackson Barlow. *The Bill of Rights and Beyond*. Washington, D.C.: Commission on the Bicentennial of the United States, Government Printing Office, 1991.

Bowen, Catherine Drinker. *Miracle at Philadelphia*. Boston: Little Brown and Company, 1966.

Chidsey, Donald Barr. *The Birth of the Constitution*. New York: Crown Publishers, 1966.

Franklin, Paula A. *The Fourth Amendment*. Englewood Cliffs, N.J.: Silver Burdett Press, Inc., 1991.

Hauptly, Denis J. *A Convention of Delegates—The Creation of the Constitution*. New York: Atheneum, 1987.

Johnson, Linda Carlson. *Our Constitution*. Brookfield, Conn.: The Millbrook Press, 1992.

Lindop, Edmund. *The Bill of Rights and Landmark Cases*. New York: Franklin Watts, 1989.

Persico, Deborah A. *Mapp v. Ohio: Evidence and Search Warrants*. Springfield, N.J.: Enslow Publishers, Inc., 1997.

Ravitch, Diane, ed. *The American Reader—Words that Moved a Nation*. New York: Harper Collins, 1990.

Ritchie, Donald A. *The U.S. Constitution*. New York: Chelsea House Publishers, 1989.

Index

A

Adams, John, 14
airport searches, 68
air searches, 65, 66, 68
Anderson v. *Creighton*, 57–58
Articles of Confederation, 16–18
automobile exception, 36, 38, 43, 78

B

Benson, Egbert, 21–22
Bill of Rights, 18–20, 22, 24, 27, 92
Boyd v. *United States*, 29–30
British Parliament, 13, 15
Burdeau v. *McDowell*, 35
Burford, Ex Parte, 24–25
Burger, Warren, 49
Byars v. *United States*, 40

C

California v. *Ciraolo*, 65–66
California v. *Hodari D.*, 56
Carroll doctrine, 38, 43, 78
Carroll v. *United States*, 36, 38
Constitution of the United States, 18–19, 21, 23
Coolidge v. *New Hampshire*, 48

D

Declaration of Independence, 15
Douglas, William O., 47
drug courier profile, 68, 69
drug-sniffing dog searches, 81, 83
drug testing in public schools, 83–85

E

Eighteenth Amendment, 31
exclusionary rule, 31–34, 45–46, 48–49

F

federal court system, 23
Fifth Amendment, 30, 60
Florida v. *Riley*, 66

G

general warrants, 11–13
Gerry, Elbridge, 18–20
good faith error exception, 51–52
Gouled v. *United States*, 35

H

Hamilton, Alexander, 17
Harlan, John Marshall, 63

I

Illinois v. *Gates*, 50
inevitable discovery exception, 50–51
innocent person search, 56
invalid warrant, 48

J

Jackson, Ex parte, 28–29
Jefferson, Thomas, 15, 18

K

Katz v. *United States*, 63

L

Locke v. *United States*, 26

M

Madison, James, 17, 20
Mapp v. *Ohio*, 45–49
Marshall, John, 25–26

Mason, George, 18–19
Massachusetts v. *Sheppard*, 52
mere evidence rule, 34–35
Murray's Lessee v. *Hoboken Land Co.*, 28

N

Nix v. *Williams*, 50–51

O

Oliver v. *United States*, 64–65
Olmstead v. *United States*, 59–60, 63
Open Fields Doctrine, 64–65
Otis, James, 13–14

P

personal searches, 71–73
personal searches of students, 78–81
private person search, 35–36

Q

qualified immunity, 57

R

Randolph, Edmund, 19

S

school locker searches, 75–78
search and seizure at sea, 41–43
Shays' Rebellion, 16–17
Sherman, Roger, 18
Sibron v. *New York*, 54
Silver Platter Doctrine, 38–40
Smith v. *Maryland*, 26–27
stop and frisk rule, 52
suspicionless drug testing, 73–74

T

Taft, William Howard, 60–61
Terry v. *Ohio*, 52–53
T.L.O. v. *New Jersey*, 7–10, 85–86
Twenty-First Amendment, 43

two-pronged Test, 47–48, 50

U

United States Court of Appeals, 23
United States District Court, 23
United States House of Representatives, 18, 20–21, 23, 93–95
United States v. *Lee*, 41–43
United States v. *Leon*, 51
United States Senate, 18, 22, 95–96
United States v. *Sokolow*, 68–70
United States Supreme Court, 18, 23–25,

V

Vernonia School District v. *Acton*, 83–84
Virginia Constitution and Declaration of Rights 18

W

Weeks v. *United States*, 31–33
White, Byron, 86
Winston v. *Lee*, 72–73
Wolf v. *Colorado*, 44–45
writs of assistance, 13–14